MATHEMATICS ON THE INTERNET

A Resource for K–12 Teachers

2nd Edition

Jerry A. Ameis
University of Winnipeg

Jazlin V. Ebenezer, Series Editor
University of Manitoba

D0920116

Upper Saddle River, New Jersey
Columbus, Ohio

Library of Congress Cataloging-in-Publication Data

Ameis, Jerry A.
    Mathematics on the Internet: a resource for K-12 teachers/Jerry A. Ameis–2nd ed
        p. cm.
    Includes bibiographical references.
    ISBN 0-13-061895-0
        1. Mathematics–Study and teaching–Computer network resources. 2. Internet in
education. I. Title.

QA11.5–A64 2002
025.06'51–dc21   2001034508

Vice President and Publisher: Jeffery W. Johnston
Editor: Linda Ashe Montgomery
Production Editor: Mary M. Irvin
Design Coordinator: Diane Lorenzo
Production Supervision and Text Design: Carlisle Publishers Services
Cover Design: Jason Moore
Cover Photo: Photodisc
Production Manager: Pamela D. Bennett
Director of Marketing: Kevin Flanagan
Marketing Manager: Krista Groshong
Marketing Coordinator: Barbara Koontz

This book was set in Minion by Carlisle Communications, Ltd., and was printed and bound
by R.R. Donnelley & Sons Company. The cover was printed by Phoenix Color Corp.

Pearson Education Ltd., *London*
Pearson Education Australia PTY, Limited, *Sydney*
Pearson Education Singapore, Pte. Ltd.
Pearson Education North Asia Ltd., *Hong Kong*
Pearson Education Canada, Ltd., *Toronto*
Pearson Educación de Mexico, S.A. de C.V.
Pearson Education—Japan, *Tokyo*
Pearson Education Malaysia, Pte. Ltd
Pearson Education, *Upper Saddle River, New Jersey*

10 9 8 7 6 5 4 3
ISBN 0-13-061895-0

To Fran, my Internet-saturated wife, for her patience and shoulder.

To my two children, Dustin (age 9) and Amanda (age 12), for their help in selecting child-friendly sites.

Preface

The Internet can be a spark for changing and shaping students' opportunities for learning mathematics. In that regard, this book helps teacher educators, college students preparing to become mathematics teachers, and teachers in elementary, middle, and secondary schools to become better acquainted with some of the resource materials and information available on the Internet to support the teaching and learning of mathematics.

All websites described in this book have been carefully reviewed to ensure that they are useful and of sufficient quality. The sites were functional at the time of writing; however, it is impossible to guarantee that the sites will remain functional over time.

Chapter 1 is intended to help you become Internet literate. It describes briefly what the Internet is and how to access information found on it. A short tutorial is included to help you learn how to use *Yahoo!*, a search directory, to search for mathematics education sites. A list of Internet tutorial sites is also provided. The sites are useful for learning how to surf the Net.

Chapter 2 is the heart of this book. It provides substantial guidance on the learning of mathematics through a discussion of teaching scenarios that involve the Internet. It discusses issues with past mathematics instructional practices and provides a view of teaching mathematics for the twenty-first century that is based on the National Council of Teachers of Mathematics (NCTM) *Principles and Standards for School Mathematics.* The chapter discusses in some detail how the Internet can be used to support the learning of mathematics. That discussion helps to clarify how to use the Internet as an instructional tool in ways that reflect current reform in teaching mathematics.

Chapter 3 is the main website directory of this book. It lists a wealth of websites containing resources that are consistent with the NCTM *Principles and Standards.* Student and practicing teachers will find these resources useful for teaching mathematics.

The sites listed in Chapter 3 are organized into six categories that directly concern the daily teaching needs of teachers. The categories are:

- Lessons and Activities (sites that provide ideas for lessons/activities)
- Problems (sites that provide problems for students to solve)
- Mathematics Content (sites that provide information on mathematics itself)
- Statistics (sites that provide access to numerical data or that involve resources for teaching statistics)
- Comprehensive Gateways (sites that provide links to a multitude of education sites)

- Other Math-Related Matters (sites that provide resources that do not fit readily into the above categories)

Each site listing includes a description and a profile consisting of eight components: intended audience, grade level, curricular fit, type of resources, authorship of site, navigation, visual appeal, and interactive activity.

Chapter 4 is also a directory chapter. It is devoted to websites that concern the professional development needs of teachers. These sites are organized into six categories:

- Associations, Organizations, Projects, Centers (sites that provide access to and information on a variety of professional development concerns)
- Information on Reform (sites that provide information on various aspects of reform in mathematics education)
- Information on Assessment (sites that provide information on assessing the mathematical understandings and skills of students)
- Collaboration (sites that facilitate collaboration and communication among teachers)
- Gender Concerns (sites that provide information on addressing gender issues in mathematics education)
- Multicultural and Minority Groups Concerns (sites that provide information on addressing multicultural and minority group issues in mathematics education)

Descriptions are provided for professional development sites, but profiles are not included.

Appendix A is an annotated list of electronic journals that pertain to teaching mathematics. Appendix B is a glossary of terms associated with the Internet.

Acknowledgments

A sincere thanks to Scott Wellman, Faculty of Education, University of Manitoba, for the technical assistance that he has provided. A sincere thanks to John Anchan, Faculty of Education, University of Winnipeg, for his helpful advice. Thanks also to the reviewers of the manuscript for their insights and comments: David Reid, Acadia University; Anne L. Madsen, University of New Mexico; Anna O. Graeber, University of Maryland; Jay Graening, University of Kansas; Dennis Showers, SUNY at Geneseo; and Steven W. Ziebarth, Western Michigan University.

Jerry A. Ameis, Ph. D.
Jazlin V. Ebenezer, Ed. D.

CONTENTS

CHAPTER 1: ■ *Using the Internet 1*

What Is the Internet? 2
What Is an Information Server? 2
What Is a URL? 3
How Do You Find Information on the Internet? 4
    Wandering Around by Clicking on Hot Spots 5
    Connecting to a Website with a URL 5
    Using a Search Engine or a Search Directory 6
Downloading Information from the Internet 10
Websites for Internet Guides and Tutorials 10
Chapter Summary 11
References 11

CHAPTER 2: ■ *Learning Mathematics with the Internet 13*

Some Issues of Mathematics Instruction 13
    Story 1 13
    Story 2 14
The NCTM *Principles and Standards* and Mathematics Instruction 14
    Reflective Writing 1 17
    Reflective Writing 2 17
The Internet and Mathematics Instruction 18
    Example 1: Locating Teaching Resources (lessons) 19
    Example 2: Locating Teaching Resources (stories) 20
    Example 3: Obtaining Assistance with Planning 22
    Example 4: Engaging Students in Simulations 23
    Example 5: Engaging students in Interactive Games 24
    Example 6: Engaging Students in Problem Solving 25
    Example 7: Engaging Students in Communicating 27
    Example 8: Engaging Students in Projects 27
Chapter Summary 28
References 28

CHAPTER 3: ■ *Links to Mathematics Teaching Resources 29*

Introduction 30
Lessons and Activities 32
    Elementary to High School Sites 33
    Elementary Grades Sites 40
    Elementary Grades and Middle Years Sites 46
    Middle Years Sites 50
    Middle Years and High School Sites 51
    High School Sites 54
Problems 58
    Elementary to High School Sites 59
    Elementary Grades Sites 63
    Elementary to Middle Years Sites 65
    Middle Years Sites 66
    Middle Years to High School Sites 68
    High School Sites 69
Mathematics Content 72
    Elementary to High School Sites 72
    Middle Years to High School Sites 76
    High School Sites 80
Statistics 85
    Elementary to High School Sites 86
    Elementary Grades Sites 89
    Middle Years to High School Sites 91
    High School Sites 92
Comprehensive Gateways 94
    Elementary to High School Sites 95
Other Math-Related Matters 99
Chapter Summary 103

CHAPTER 4: ■ *Links to Professional Development Resources 104*

Associations, Organizations, Projects, Centers 105
Information on Reform 110
Information on Assessment 113

Collaboration 116
Gender Concerns 118
Multicultural and Minority Groups Concerns 121
Chapter Summary 124

APPENDIX A

Electronic Journals 125

APPENDIX B

The Internet Language 127

CHAPTER 1

Using the Internet

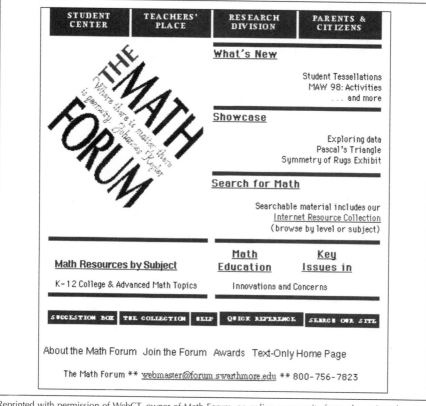

STUDENT CENTER	TEACHERS' PLACE	RESEARCH DIVISION	PARENTS & CITIZENS

What's New

Student Tessellations
MAW 98: Activities
. . . and more

Showcase

Exploring data
Pascal's Triangle
Symmetry of Rugs Exhibit

Search for Math

Searchable material includes our
Internet Resource Collection
(browse by level or subject)

Math Resources by Subject

K-12 College & Advanced Math Topics

Math Education

Innovations and Concerns

Key Issues in

SUGGESTION BOX	THE COLLECTION	HELP	QUICK REFERENCE	SEARCH OUR SITE

About the Math Forum   Join the Forum   Awards   Text-Only Home Page

The Math Forum ** webmaster@forum.swarthmore.edu ** 800-756-7823

- What is the Internet?
- What is an information server?
- What is an URL?
- How do you find information on the Internet?
- Downloading information from the Internet
- Websites for Internet guides and tutorials

WHAT IS THE INTERNET?

Imagine a large and unusual octopus that has hundreds of tentacles. Inside the octopus there are many small squid touching each other's arms. Now imagine millions of these octopuses hanging onto each other's tentacles. This network of connected octopuses and squids gives you an idea of the nature of the Internet. It is a huge network of interconnected computer networks and computers linking the whole world.

Here is an example of how this linkage can occur: The computers in a college of education can be linked to form a network of computers called a LAN (Local Area Network). This single network of computers can then be connected to other colleges in the same university. This larger computer network is then connected to other university networks, school networks, government networks, business and industry networks, and private homes in a country and other countries (see Figure 1-1). The effect is to create an enormous web of linked computers and computer networks that transcends geographical barriers.

The Internet is, in effect, a network of networks. The linked computers and networks that comprise it communicate with each other through such means as regular telephone lines, fiber optic lines, and satellite transmissions. Although the linked computers often are of different types (e.g., Macintosh or IBM), they send data to each other through a common language called Transmission Control Protocol/Internet Protocol (TCP/IP).

This enormous capacity to send and receive data across the globe provides us with an unparalleled freedom to communicate with each other in a variety of ways. We can communicate through electronic mail (e-mail). We can communicate "in living color" through real-time live video and sound transmissions. We can communicate through rich multimedia documents consisting of text, graphics, and even sound, or through simple documents consisting only of text. Documents found on the Internet can be stored as files on the hard drives of our own computers through a process known as downloading. Downloaded documents can be modified and printed for our own purposes by using, for example, word processing software.

WHAT IS AN INFORMATION SERVER?

An information server is something like a warehouse that holds and distributes information. Information on the Internet is stored and transmitted by information servers which are special computers that have a large data storage capacity (see Figure 1-1). Information servers are operated by companies/organizations known generally as Internet service providers (ISP). Websites (home pages and their accompanying files) are stored on these information servers.

There are different types of information servers: *http, gopher,* and *archie.* These servers present information in different layouts and styles. Http servers can

Figure 1-1   The Internet

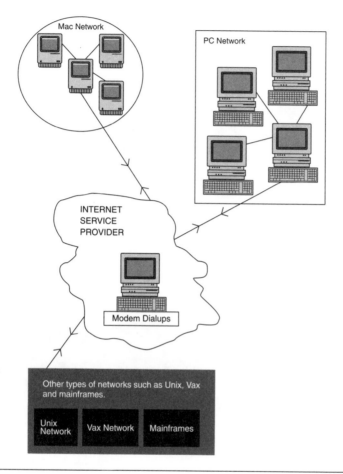

present information as multimedia documents (text, sound, graphics, and movies). In contrast, gopher and archie servers can only present text-based information. Http servers are the dominant type of server.

WHAT IS A URL?

Each website stored on a server has its own address called a URL (Uniform Resource Locator). A URL is similar to a house address except that it is the address of a bundle of information stored on an information server. An example of a URL for a website is: **http://www.stritch.edu/~math/resources.html**.

Table 1-1	Zones and What They represent

Zone	Representation
com	commercial organization
edu	educational organization or institution
mil	military-related site
net	network organization
org	professional group or organization
int	international organization or association
gov	government organization or agency
ca	name of a country (ca: Canada)

The standard format for a URL is **protocol://host.domain[:port][/path][filename]** in which:

■ the *protocol* is http (HyperText Transport Protocol) for an http type of information server.

■ *host.domain* is a reference to the server (in the case of the example: **www.stritch.edu**).

■ *path* is a reference to the website on the server (in the case of the example: **~math**).

■ *filename* is a reference to a file in the site (in the case of the example: **resources.html**).

It is possible to obtain additional information about the site from its URL. Part of the URL is a zone designation (see Table 1-1). Some common zones are in bold-face in the sample URLs below:

http://www.macromedia.**com**

http://www.umanitoba.**ca**

http://instruct.cms.uncwil.**edu**

HOW DO YOU FIND INFORMATION ON THE INTERNET?

Looking for information on the Internet (surfing the Net) requires a special kind of software called a browser. Internet browsers such as Netscape Navigator/ Communicator and Microsoft Explorer provide a way to find and access websites that contain information you are seeking. There are three basic ways to find information: (1) wandering around by clicking on hot spots, (2) connecting to a website with a URL, and (3) using a search engine such as HotBot, or a search directory such as Yahoo.

Wandering Around by Clicking on Hot Spots

A browser connects you to a website when you use the mouse to click on a hot spot on the web page you are looking at. The hot spots can be active buttons or parts of maps or blue underlined text. The dominant kind of hot spot is blue underlined text. When a browser detects a mouse click on a hot spot, it finds the website that is linked to that hot spot and displays the opening web page of that website. Note that sometimes a browser will be unable to connect to a website. This can happen for a variety of reasons (for example, the website may no longer be active).

Connecting to a Website with a URL

The following instructions apply to Netscape Navigator/Communicator. Some of the user input details may vary according to the version of Navigator/Communicator being used. Note that other browsers such as Microsoft Explorer require similar steps to follow.

Step 1.   Launch the browser application (Netscape Navigator/Communicator in this case).

Step 2.   Type the URL of the website in the "Open location" box (by clicking the *Open* button or by selecting "Open location" found in the file menu). See Figure 1-2.

Step 3.   Press *Return* or click on the *Open* button. You will be connected to the website unless it is inactive or too busy to respond at the moment (because of too much traffic at the site). In either case, Navigator/ Communicator will provide an explanation for a failed connection.

Figure 1-2   An Open Location Box

Table 1-2 URLs for Some Search Engine Sites

Search Engine	URL
Altavista	http://www.altavista.com/
Excite	http://www.excite.com/
HotBot	http://hotbot.lycos.com/
Infoseek	http://www.infoseek.com/

Using a Search Engine or a Search Directory

Search engines and search directories allow you to harness, to some degree, the abundance of websites that are on the Internet (the number of sites is in the millions and rapidly growing). By using search engines and directories involving definitive subject and topic searches, information and resources can be located relatively quickly and then extracted. Different search engines and directories can produce different search results. This is because they can differ in the way searches make use of key words and also because of differences in the databases being searched.

Search engines (see Table 1-2) create listings of websites automatically. Search engines "crawl" the web by means of tools called spiders that visit web pages and read the contents on a regular basis. The results are stored in a catalog, a giant electronic book that contains a copy of every web page the spider finds. If a web page is changed, the spider updates the page in the catalog. Search engine software sifts through the pages stored in the catalog to find matches to search words and ranks the matches in order of relevance. The ranking depends primarily on two factors: whether a search word appears in the title of the website, and the frequency that a search word appears throughout the site. Reading the "hints" and "help" for each search engine will explain how the search tool operates.

There also are specialized search engines that perform meta-searches (see Table 1-3). Such engines look for matches to search words within search engines

Table 1-3 URLs for Some Meta-Search Sites

Meta-Search Engine	URL
Ask Jeeves	http://www.askjeeves.com/
DogPile	http://www.dogpile.com/
MetaCrawler	http://www.metacrawler.com/

Table 1-4	URLs for Some Search Directory Sites

Search Engine	URL
About.com	http://www.about.com/
Galaxy	http://galaxy.einet.net/galaxy.html
Magellan	http://www.mckinley.com/
Yahoo!	http://www.yahoo.com/

themselves. In effect, meta-search engines search the searchers. A drawback to meta-searching is that it can be slow. It is most effective when performing a specific one-word search.

Search directories (see Table 1-4) depend on people for the listings. Websites are included in the listing of a search directory in one or both of two basic ways: (1) website creators submit a short description to a directory, or (2) search directory editors select and categorize websites for inclusion in a directory.

Suppose that you want to find mathematics lesson plans. The words "K-12 mathematics lessons" seem to be reasonable search words to use. Having decided on your search words, it is time to start the search. Our example uses Yahoo! (**http://www.yahoo.com/**).

Click on the "Education" category of Yahoo!. Note that you can simply enter your search words, but preselecting a category can reduce search time. Many subcategories are listed at the Education category. You could select the subcategory "Math and Science Education" but instead enter the search words.

Enter "K-12 mathematics lessons" and click on *Search*. The search results will appear. When we wrote this book there were 13 hits with **Columbia Education Center's Mini Lessons** at the top of the list (your search results may differ now). Click on that link. This takes you to the Columbia Education Center page "CEC Lesson Plans."

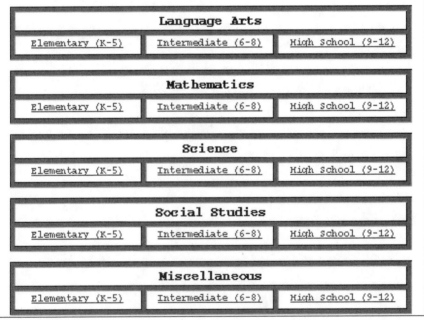

Courtesy of Columbia Education Center

CEC Lesson Plans.
http://www.col-ed.org/cur/

Suppose you are interested in mathematics lessons for the intermediate (6-8) level. Click on that link. When we wrote this book that took us to "Mathematics Lesson Plans."

Mathematics Lesson Plans

Math - Elementary (K-5)

math01.txt   Math review on concept and facts (4-6)
math02.txt   Learning multiplication tables (2-6)
math03.txt   Interpret data and making a graph (3-6)
math04.txt   Exploring Base 4 (4)
math05.txt   One to one matching and writing numerals (K-1)
math06.txt   Calculator Pattern Puzzles (gifted K-5)
math07.txt   Observation, sorting, predicting, using valentine candy
(1-4)
math08.txt   Use of manipulatives to Pre-Algebra (3-8)
math09.txt   Making Change; Buying at community store (K-2)
math10.txt   Multiplication; hands-on arrays, skip counting (2-3)
math13.txt   Using M&M cookies to work math problems (4-6)
math14.txt   Addition and Subtraction game (2-8)
math16.txt   Place Value using a dice game (4)
math17.txt   Ratio; using peanut butter & jelly sandwich (4-6)
math18.txt   Mystery number motivates place value (2-6)
math19.txt   Fraction Hunt activity sheet (3-5)
math20.txt   Cooking; practical application of math (4-6)
math21.txt   Making estimations (2)
math24.txt   Estimation using grocery list (3-5)
math25.txt   Problem solving using the sports page (4)
math26.txt   Probability with hands-on/cooperative learning activity
(1-5)
math27.txt   "Math Shortcuts"; multiplication & division (4-6)
math30.txt   Area & Volume; a hands-on activity (3-6)
math32.txt   Tree Measurement: Understanding vertical and horizontal
measurement of large objects (4-6)
math33.txt   Problem Solving and Computation activity using pattern
blocks (1-3)
math39.txt   Equivalent Fractions, easily identified using physical
objects (3-5)
math40.txt   Thinking Skill activity using '21 Game' (2-6)
math43.txt   Positive and Negative numbers activity (4- 12)
math44.txt   Listening Practice/Team Review activity (4- 8)
math45.txt   "Estimating With Money", (1-5)
math49.txt   "Multiplication Bingo", (3-5)
math50.txt   "Number Tick-Tack-Toe", practice addition facts (1-3)

CEC / SMCNWS Webmaster

Mathematics Lesson Plans
http://www.col-ed.org/cur/math.html#math1

Suppose you are interested in a lesson about equivalent fractions. Click on the link (**math54.txt**). A lesson entitled "Equivalent Fractions Game" is displayed. All that remains is to decide whether or not the lesson is appropriate, remembering that it might need modification to suit the learning needs of your students. If the lesson is appropriate, you can download and modify it before making hard copies for your students.

DOWNLOADING INFORMATION FROM THE INTERNET

It is possible to download information found on the Internet to your hard drive or to another computer disk. The downloaded information is stored as a file that can be accessed by you in a variety of ways. For example, you can download a mathematics problem, saving it as a file. Open that file with your word processing software (for example, Microsoft Word), modify the problem to suit your needs, and then print a hard copy of it so that you can photocopy the problem for your students. The Internet would be far less useful if it did not allow for the downloading of information as files.

To download information, select the *Save as* feature found on your browser in the file menu. Enter a name for the file and indicate where to store it (on your hard drive or another disk). Unfortunately, this procedure saves only the text portion of the information. It does not save any graphics (images) that might be part of the information. Graphics need to be separately saved as files using a different procedure.

To save a graphic, place the pointer (the cursor) on the graphic and press and hold down the mouse button. A menu pops up. Select the option *Save this image as*. Enter a name for the file and indicate where to store it (on your hard drive or another computer disk). You need to repeat the procedure for each graphic you wish to save.

WEBSITES FOR INTERNET GUIDES AND TUTORIALS

Guides and tutorials are available on the Internet to help in using it. The following annotated listing provides information on sites whose major purpose is to assist Internet users.

Title of Site: Ask Dr. Internet
URL: http://promo.net/drnet

This site has an extensive archive that provides answers to frequently asked questions (FAQs) about the Web. You also can submit your own questions.

Title of Site: Internet 101
URL: http://www2.famvid.com/i101/

This site provides basic information on using the Internet, including tips on searching and on using e-mail, newsgroup, and chat services.

Title of Site: "WHAT CAN I DO TO BE NET SAFE."
URL: http://www.ou.edu/oupd/kidsafe/inet.htm

This site provides a step-by-step on-line tutorial and instructions on how children can use the Internet safely.

Title of Site: The New Users Directory
URL: http://hcs.harvard.edu/~calvarez/newuser.html

This Harvard University site gives an introductory overview of the Web. It features a simple guide on how to download software and provides links to other starting points.

CHAPTER SUMMARY

This chapter provides an overview of the Internet to help the reader understand what the Internet is and how to begin to locate and extract information contained on it. Additional information is available by accessing the guide and tutorial websites listed in this chapter and by examining the appendices of this book.

References

Search Engine Watch; Tips about Internet Searches.
  http://www.searchenginewatch.com/index.html
Turlington, S. R. (1999). *The unauthorized guide to the internet.* Indianapolis, IN: Que Corporation.

CHAPTER 2

Learning Mathematics with the Internet

Welcome to MathMagic on the Web!

- All About MathMagic:
  - What is MathMagic?
  - How do I Participate?
  - About the Lists
  - Of Particular Benefit to Teachers: Discussions
  - Registration/Participation: Details
  - How do I subscribe/unsubscribe? Instructions
  - Who can answer more questions? More Info
  - Adult involvement
  - Meet MrH
  - Meet some of the teams
- Current Challenges:
  - K-3
  - 4-6

Courtesy of Alan A. Hodson

MathMagic on the Web
http://forum.swarthmore.edu/mathmagic/

- Some Issues of Mathematics Instruction
- The NCTM *Principles and Standards* and Mathematics Instruction
- The Internet and Mathematics Instruction

SOME ISSUES OF MATHEMATICS INSTRUCTION

More than a decade has passed since the publication of two seminal documents—*Everybody counts: A report to the nation on the future of mathematics education* (National Research Council, 1989) and *Curriculum and Evaluation Standards for School Mathematics* (NCTM, 1989). Each document strongly urged improvement in the teaching and learning of mathematics and the evidence suggests that important progress has been made since then.

For example, Martinez and Martinez (1998) commented that more students are taking mathematics; the gap between white and minority achievement in mathematics is narrowing; and assessment data indicates that students' learning of mathematics is increasing. However, there are still too many classrooms where reform is not being implemented in any significant way; it is largely in these classrooms that insufficient progress seems to be occurring.

The reader may ask if reform in mathematics education actually is needed; it is a reasonable question. The stories of two preservice (student) teachers who were enrolled in a K-6 mathematics curriculum and instruction course (Ameis, 1997) might shed some light on this issue. As part of the course, the preservice teachers shared their own past mathematical learning experiences. Each of the following stories is about one of those experiences. The reader may have a similar story to tell.

Story 1

When I first began learning basic arithmetic in elementary school, I did not experience any anxieties until grade 3, when I began multiplying 2 digit numbers. From then until high school, I had a lot of trouble with math, and it seemed to define my intelligence to my teachers. I was not allowed to say that it was "too hard," and was often yelled at if I did. In junior high, I finally began to realize that if I wanted to get through math, I would have to use a different talent of mine: memorization. After memorizing formulas and algorithms, math began to be more tolerable, and my grades skyrocketed into the top ten of my class.

While my grades were improving in high school, I never really gave much thought to how my mind was grasping the concepts of math. It felt good to finally have the pressure of "understanding" math taken off of me, but it never occurred to me that I did not really understand it. When I began having to take care of my own expenses, I noticed that I had difficulty applying all the algorithms and formulas that I had so cleverly "learned" in school to real life. I had a very difficult time with simple calculations and simple applications of concepts.

Upon reflection, I think that I took a very passive stance in my mathematics education. I was not empowered at all in my education; rather, I gave the teacher what he or she asked for, without any thought to my own understanding. I did not know what I was learning, nor did I know why I was learning it.

Story 2

In public school, I was never under the impression that math was an enjoyable thing to do. In fact, I dreaded having to sit and do math each day. Adding, subtracting, and multiplying never really disagreed with me, but when we began long division, I was against math completely. Sitting down and working through a long division problem was like having to stay at the dinner table until your piece of liver was gone—it was pure torture, but you knew, deep down that not finishing it would cause some major upheaval in the Force and the world would no longer continue (not a very pleasant thought for my young mind).

And yet I was never a bad student - even in math I always pulled off good grades. I could do the work but the problem lay in the fact that I never learned the reasons behind the equations. No one ever bothered giving me a reason as to why I had to be able to figure out how many groups of ducks could fit into the area of a football field. It didn't seem to have a point, and no one seemed to have very much fun doing it. I wanted to gain knowledge that I could use but math rarely offered that to me. And so in grade 12, I had a party right after "the last math class in my life".

The two stories provide insight into some of the issues pertaining to mathematics education. A common thread running through them is the importance of understanding the mathematics being taught and of having a reason for learning the mathematics. Other issues also are touched on in the stories: evaluation that focuses on the regurgitation of formulas and algorithms, the appreciation of mathematics as a creative human endeavor, and the development of problem-solving skills that can be applied to real-life situations.

Stories like these reveal some of the reasons why organizations such as the National Council of Teachers of Mathematics (NCTM) continue to promote reform in mathematics education.

THE NCTM *PRINCIPLES AND STANDARDS* AND MATHEMATICS INSTRUCTION

Because it is essential that reform in mathematics education remain vital and current, the original NCTM *Standards* (1989) has been revised. The revision is entitled *Principles and Standards for School Mathematics* (NCTM, 2000). It takes into account new learning technologies (for example: the Internet was largely a gleam in someone's eye in 1989), new information about how students learn mathematics, and new approaches to reforming mathematics education that were gained during the years of work with the NCTM *Standards*. While the revision includes necessary changes, the central message of the original *Standards* is still preserved, namely, that all students deserve a high-quality mathematics education.

Principles and Standards for School Mathematics (NCTM, 2000) promotes six principles:

- The Equity Principle: Excellence in mathematics education requires high expectations and strong support for all students.
- The Curriculum Principle: A curriculum must be coherent, focused on important mathematics, and well articulated across the grades.
- The Teaching Principle: Effective mathematics teaching requires understanding what students know and need to learn and then challenging and supporting them to learn it well.
- The Learning Principle: Students must learn mathematics with understanding, actively building new knowledge from experience and prior knowledge.
- The Assessment Principle: Assessment should support the learning of important mathematics and furnish useful information to both students and teachers.
- The Technology Principle: Technology is essential in teaching and learning mathematics; it influences the mathematics that is taught and enhances students' learning.

These principles permeate the standards. A standard describes an area of mathematical focus that students should be learning and using. The document includes both content and process standards.

There are five content standards:

- Number and Operations
- Algebra
- Geometry
- Measurement
- Data Analysis and Probability.

Each content standard explicitly describes at least several focus areas for mathematics instruction. For example, Content Standard 2 (Algebra) states that algebra is more than manipulating symbols. Students need to understand the concepts of algebra, the structure and the principles that govern the manipulation of symbols, and how the symbols can be used for recording ideas and for gaining insight into problem situations. Content Standard 2 begins in the early years when students work with patterns and representations.

There are five process standards as well:

- Problem Solving
- Reasoning and Proof
- Communication
- Connections
- Representation.

The process standards suggest ways of acquiring and using mathematical content knowledge. For example, one aspect of Process Standard 2 (Reasoning and Proof) concerns students making and investigating mathematical conjectures where conjecture is a major pathway to discovering insight into mathematics. The reader can refer to the website, **http://www.nctm.org/standards/**, for further information on *Principles and Standards for School Mathematics.*

An example of what the standards might look like in practice is useful at this point. The example involves preservice teachers themselves learning mathematics in a way that is consistent with the principles and standards discussed in *Principles and Standards for School Mathematics.* Such mathematical learning was a preliminary part of the K-6 mathematics curriculum and instruction course taught by J. A. Ameis (1997).

In order for the preservice teachers to experience a mathematical learning situation that is comparable to that experienced by children in schools, the preservice teachers worked with mathematical materials and ideas that were unfamiliar to them, including the Chinese abacus. The mathematical goals for working with the abacus were to represent numbers on it and to do arithmetic $(+, -, \times, \div)$ with it.

The goals could have been addressed by show-and-tell teaching. The instructor could have demonstrated how to represent numbers on the abacus and then provided tasks that involved practice with representing numbers. While this would have involved using concrete materials (the Chinese abacus is a concrete material), simply working with concrete materials is not sufficient for instructional practice that seeks to reflect *Principles and Standards for School Mathematics.*

Rather than using show-and-tell teaching, however, the instructor used a teaching approach that involved problem solving and discovery. Achieving the mathematical goals became, in effect, a problem for the preservice teachers to solve. The students were asked to form small groups and to use the Chinese abacus to represent "26" in whatever way made sense to them. The solutions were shared and discussed. No group represented 26 in the "Chinese" way (the one involving place value: the elegant and efficient way; see Figure 2-1), yet all of their solutions did make sense. For example, one group decided that each upper bead

Figure 2-1   An Abbreviated Chinese Abacus with 26 Represented on It.

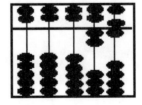

was worth five and each lower bead one. To represent 26, they pushed up five upper beads and one lower bead ($5 \times 5 + 1 = 26$).

After their invented ways of representing numbers on the abacus had been shared and discussed, the instructor then could have proceeded by having the preservice teachers apply those ways to doing arithmetic on the abacus. However, that would have involved deviating from the intent of *Principles and Standards for School Mathematics,* namely, that the mathematics being learned should be significant and ultimately should be correct from the point of view of external criteria. Their invented ways of representing numbers were clumsy in relation to what was required for doing nontrivial arithmetic. For that reason, applying those ways to doing arithmetic significantly would have limited the depth and scope of their arithmetic thinking and their understandings of the abacus.

Instead, the instructor asked the preservice teachers to use their invented ways to represent the number 234,508,412. This task caused them to think about other ways to represent numbers on the abacus because none of their previous ways was adequate for the new task. Eventually, the way involving place value understandings emerged and was reinforced by discussion and practice. After efficient number representation on the abacus was understood, the preservice teachers learned how to do arithmetic on it. The teaching approach used was similar to that for representing numbers.

The preservice teachers reflected on their learning with the abacus after the first class. Here are two samples that are typical of what they wrote.

Reflective Writing 1

When we worked with the abacus in class I noticed how you presented us with a problem and then gave us the opportunity to work with it, form ideas, and come up with possible solutions. I like how you gave us time to explore before we were given hints by other classmates or yourself. I think it is also good that we were allowed to share opinions on alternatives to the solution presented. This is a definite shift from the math I have known. It is unlike anything I have seen before. It is more interesting and challenging than the math programs I was offered in elementary and high school. For the first time in math I have been allowed to experience problem solving and think for myself rather than having a teacher show me how to obtain a certain solution. This is the type of math that people can really learn from.

Reflective Writing 2

One aspect of class that I am finding particularly interesting is the investigative approach. Having students think in this way challenges them to understand what they are doing. On our first day of class when we used the abacus, I didn't have a clue how to represent a number on it. I know that I have explored this concept at least once before in previous math classes but I could not recall the information needed to solve the problem in front of me. When I was allowed to explore and test my hypothesis on the abacus I discovered it didn't work. My previous notions or misinformation about an abacus were dispelled as I got to experiment with the proper method. This is information that I will not forget because it was an enjoyable, hands-on activity. Also being able to talk to others and learn about the ways that they chose to solve the problem was very enlightening. As future teachers we need to be aware of different thoughts and views that our students have and how we can guide them to find the path to success.

These reflective writings indicate that the preservice teachers appreciated the learning power of a teaching approach that involved the process standards found in the NCTM *Principles and Standards*. The teaching approach invited the preservice teachers to problem solve collaboratively, to reason and explain their reasoning, and to communicate their reasoning. Experiencing these processes helped them to realize that when learning mathematics involves active "minds-on" participation by learners, the mathematics being learned becomes more meaningful and more deeply learned.

THE INTERNET AND MATHEMATICS INSTRUCTION

The Technology Principle of *Principles and Standards for School Mathematics* (NCTM, 2000) clearly states that technology such as the Internet is not a panacea for the challenges inherent in teaching mathematics or a cure for ineffective teaching practice. Nor is the Internet a replacement for basic mathematical understandings and skills that students need to gain. Rather, the Internet can be used to foster those understandings and skills and enrich students' learning of mathematics.

The Internet can be used as an instructional tool in ways that are consistent with *Principles and Standards for School Mathematics*. The Internet offers teachers resources for teaching important areas of mathematics and offers students opportunities to engage the interrelated processes of investigation, reflection, communication, problem solving, and reasoning. For example, there are websites that present curriculum-specific problems to solve and that encourage students to communicate and share their reasoning about their solutions to the problems.

The process standard, Problem Solving, of *Principles and Standards for School Mathematics* indicates that learning proceeds best when it arises out of problem situations. The Internet can offer those situations or enhance them. For example, there are websites that provide relevant and current numerical data that can lead students to ask and investigate such questions as: How do the daily temperatures for cities in the United States compare to those for cities in other countries? Addressing these kinds of questions would require students to use and/or to learn data management skills.

Using the Internet to support the teaching and learning of mathematics requires a shift in thinking on the part of teachers and students if the Internet's potential for assisting in worthwhile learning is going to be realized. The shift for teachers concerns becoming a facilitator and mentor, someone who challenges and motivates students to think about and use mathematics and who assists them as necessary. The shift for students concerns taking more ownership of their own learning. In doing so, students will take on an active role in constructing their own knowledge rather than passively wait for teachers to reveal the desired or required mathematical truths.

It needs to be said that if the Internet is used in ways that are not consistent with *Principles and Standards for School Mathematics,* then its impact on learning is likely to be significantly restricted. To put it another way, using the Internet to support show-and-tell teaching would be something like placing a blanket over a television set and having the viewers just listen to the sound.

Some detail is needed to help the reader better understand how the Internet can be used as an instructional tool. Eight examples are provided below for that purpose. They should make it clearer how the Internet can be incorporated into classroom practice so as to support worthwhile mathematical learning.

Example 1: Locating Teaching Resources (Lessons)

Perhaps the most obvious use for the Internet is as a source of interesting and worthwhile teaching resources such as lesson plans, activities, problems, projects, and ideas. There are numerous websites that offer such resources. Once the desired resource has been found, it likely will require some modification to meet the specific needs of a particular teaching situation.

One approach to finding teaching resources is to make use of what are referred to in this book as *gateway sites*. These sites consist primarily of links to other sites. Here is an example of a gateway-originated search for and modification of a lesson:

The teacher (a preservice teacher in a practicum setting) was looking for a lesson on probability that would be suitable for the grade 6 class (Ameis, 1997). She e-mailed the instructor about her needs; he suggested that she begin her search with a gateway site that is now included in: **Sites for Teachers** (**http:// www.sitesforteachers.com/**).

The teacher clicked on "Math". This took her to another web page that presented a list of mathematics resources (lesson plans, ideas & activities, etc.). She selected "Lesson Plans". A long list of annotated links offered lesson plans for a variety of grade levels. She located the first link she saw for her desired grade level ("Academy Curriculum Exchange (6-8)") and clicked on it (**http://ofcn.org/ cyber.serv/academy/ace/math/inter.html**). Fortunately, a short list of only 13 lesson plans was displayed. Luck was with her even more: The second lesson on the list was "Probability using game rock, scissors, paper (5-12)".

She clicked on it and after examining the probability-related lesson plan, she sent an e-mail message to the instructor that described her classroom situation and also requested feedback on the suitability of the lesson (her message included the URL for the site). The instructor examined the lesson and posed several questions via e-mail that pertained to the appropriateness of the activities described in the lesson plan and its learning outcomes.

It turned out that the lesson plan suited her teaching needs and reflected reform in mathematics education. The lesson involved students collecting, graphing, and interpreting data. Students analyzed the game Rock, Scissors, Paper by listing possible outcomes to determine if it is fair (a theoretical model) and comparing the analysis to what actually happened when the game was played. Probability was involved in significant ways (numerically and through tree diagrams).

There was one small problem with the lesson plan, which stated that the lesson should begin by the teacher demonstrating Rock, Scissors, Paper to the students. She was aware that many of her students already knew the game and that beginning the lesson by demonstrating the game would likely be counterproductive. She modified the lesson by having students suggest games that could be investigated to see if they were fair. She expected a number of suggestions, including such ones as X's and O's. From the list of suggestions, she would then be able to steer the students to Rock, Scissors, Paper and leave some of the other ones for a later time.

Example 2: Locating Teaching Resources (Stories)

The Internet offers resources other than lesson plans for teaching mathematics. For example, some websites contain stories involving mathematics and problem solving. **Mathematical Tale Winds** is one such site. The site's resources are suitable for students in grades 2 to 5.

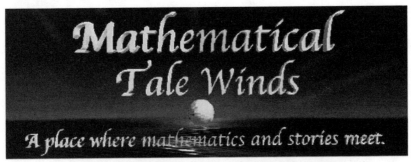

Story Resources Corner	Circle of Flame Corner
Course Info Corner	Site Info Corner
Daughter's Corner	Son's Corner

Mathematical Tale Winds
http://www.uwinnipeg.ca/~jameis/

The site contains concept stories that support the teaching of particular mathematical concepts. For example, a teacher can download a concept story such as *A day at the zoo with the D-creatures* and read it to students in an interactive way to teach the concepts of one dimension, two dimensions, and three dimensions. Students can construct the cages and the D-creature occupants in the classroom to strengthen their understanding of 1-D, 2-D, and 3-D forms.

The site also contains interesting nonroutine mathematical problems. The problems are presented as short stories set in the fantasy land of Pome whose inhabitants are pnomes (similar to gnomes). A teacher can download suitable problems and use them as part of teaching particular mathematical concepts such as number patterns.

The site contains an unusual story resource, *The Circle of Flame,* an ongoing story that has mathematical problems embedded in it. A new chapter is added to the story every couple of months. Students can read a chapter, solving the mathematical problems in it as part of a focus on problem solving that is integrated with language arts.

Mathematical Tale Winds has another feature that can encourage students to engage in mathematics. The site invites students to e-mail illustrations for the various story resources, illustrations that are then included with the site's stories. Credit is given to contributing students.

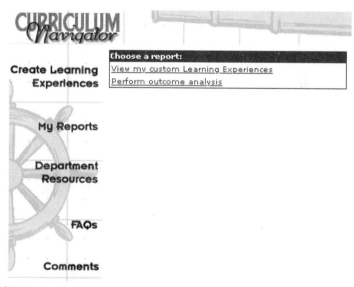

Courtesy of CITI Project, Manitoba Education

Curriculum Navigator
http://www3.edu.gov.mb.ca/cn

Example 3: Obtaining Assistance with Planning

The Internet is beginning to offer intelligent-system resources to assist teachers with planning. One site is **Curriculum Navigator**, a Manitoba Education project that integrates K-8 mathematics curricula with computer technology, including the Internet and software such as word processing, spreadsheet, and drawing applications.

The site allows teachers to locate and connect learning experiences to outcomes from Manitoba's K-8 mathematics curricula and those of the provinces and territories in the Western Canadian Protocol agreement. A learning experience is a series of teaching and assessment strategies. Teachers select teaching strategies (activating, acquiring, applying) from a learning experience based on their students' differentiated needs. The learning experiences frequently involve computer software such as paint applications or instructional programs such as *Mighty Math Carnival Countdown* or the Internet. Some websites are for teacher reference and some are for student use.

The teacher logs onto the site (http://www3.edu.gov.mb.ca/newcn/login.jsp) using a password or obtains one free of charge if he/she does not yet have one. The password feature enables the site to reserve server space for each teacher accessing the site and to enable automatic tracking of the outcomes associated with the chosen learning experiences. These learning experiences can be printed and/or saved as a report file on the site's server for future reference. The teacher's report file is password-protected.

The search provides a list of titles of learning experiences that are viewed individually. Learning experiences always contain:

- Teaching strategies
- A list of mathematics curriculum outcomes addressed by the learning experiences
- Assessment suggestions
- An estimate of the time needed for each learning experience
- A notepad for adding personalized notes.

and may contain:

- BLM's: Files or templates that may be downloaded to support instruction. The files can be edited and include modifiable word processing, spreadsheet, database, or graphics files.
- Automatic inclusion of other teaching strategies that are required for a complete learning experience
- Samples demonstrating completed student work or exemplars
- Tips on mathematics and/or outcomes that provide teachers with additional instructional information and classroom management strategies
- Information technology tags that identify information technology skills and competencies integrated with the learning experiences

■ Assistance with using information technology resources (for example, a link to an on-line tutorial)

■ Links to supportive websites (for teacher reference or student use).

Teachers can customize the report generated by the site before printing it and/or saving it on the site's server. Customizing includes selecting desired teaching strategies and adding personal notes to them. The site also has a convenience button "Take Our Suggestion" that identifies core learning teaching strategies that satisfy teacher-identified outcomes. The teacher can build a report from the suggested strategies or deselect specific strategies and replace them with others. Either way, the generated report provides teachers with a useful plan for teaching mathematics.

Example 4: Engaging Students in Simulations

Simulations can be useful for engaging students in mathematical thinking and in seeing the relevance of mathematical concepts and skills. The University of Winnipeg **Mutual Fund Challenge** (**http://mutualfundchallenge.org**) offers a simulation about mutual fund investing that addresses topics such as percent and making investments from consumer mathematics. The simulation has available 3,795 Canadian mutual funds (at the time of writing this book) that can be included in the investment portfolio of a group of students.

The Mutual Fund Challenge is both a simulation and an actual realistic investment. Groups of students form a small mutual fund themselves by contributing $5 each. The teacher remits the group's pool of money to the Mutual Fund Challenge on the group's behalf and sets up a real portfolio for them with a website value worth 1,000 times the students' actual money. Students then manage their portfolio through the Mutual Fund Challenge website, buying and selling shares under the same conditions that would apply to actual mutual funds. The top ten performers are posted daily on the site, encouraging students to make informed and well-thought-out investment decisions and to estimate and calculate investment returns.

At the end of the course, each student receives a redemption check for his or her pro-rata share of the value of the group's portfolio (naturally, scaled down by a factor of 1,000). In this way, the simulated investment is connected to a student's actual investment of $5.

There is no charge for participating in the challenge. The operating expenses are covered by the TD Mutual Funds, which also offers a bonus of $50 to each member of the student group whose portfolio achieves the highest annual percentage return during an academic year.

Example 5: Engaging Students in Interactive Games

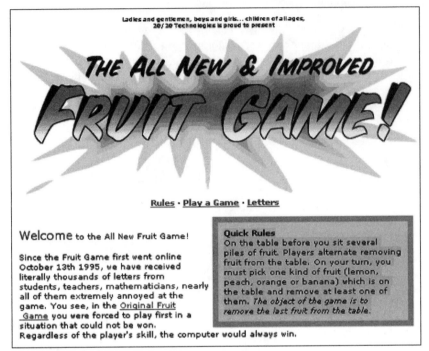

Courtesy of 20/20 Technologies

The All New & Improved Fruit Game
http://www.2020tech.com/fruit/index.html

Websites that provide interactive games can capture students' interests and motivate them to engage in mathematical learning and problem solving. **The All New & Improved Fruit Game** is one such website. It offers a variant of Nim, a game involving the removal of objects.

The Fruit Game is interactive; the student, who has the option to go first or second, plays against a computer. The student and computer alternate removing fruit from a table that has four rows of fruit on it (lemon, peach, orange, or banana). Each player must select one row and remove at least one of the fruits from it. The winner is the player who removes the last fruit from the table.

The Fruit Game is an example of an unfair game in that there is a winning strategy. If the player can determine it, he or she can beat the computer. It is this feature that offers worthwhile mathematical thinking and learning for middle years students. They can analyze simpler removal games before analyzing the Fruit Game and then examining the site's analysis of it. An example of a simpler removal game follows.

The game begins with 19 objects in one pile. Two players take turns removing 1, 2, or 3 objects from the pile in a turn. The winner is the player who removes the last object(s). There is a winning strategy for the first player. He or she should always leave the second player with a number of objects that is a multiple of four. Therefore, player #1 must begin by removing 3 objects (leaving 16 objects for player #2, a multiple of 4). Suppose that player #2 then removes 1 object. Player #1 has to remove 3 objects (leaving 12 objects for player #2). If the play continues in this way, player #1 is guaranteed to win.

Example 6: Engaging Students in Problem Solving

The following is an example that involves pairs of grade 9 students working on challenging word problems (Ameis, 1998). The teacher paired mathematically stronger students with weaker students. There were 26 students in the class. They were taking a university-oriented mathematics course.

The teacher wanted his students to become better at solving difficult word problems. He found a website that offered 50 such problems and anticipated that many of his students would be motivated to solve them.

At the start of the week, the teacher asked each pair of students to select and solve two word problems from the site: **Word Problems for Kids** (**http://www.stfx.ca/special/mathproblems/welcome.html**). The problems each pair selected had to be different from those selected by the other students (a list of selected problems was maintained). The problems and complete solutions (a complete solution consisted of detailed explanations as well as the final answer) were to be presented to the entire class by each pair over the course of several weeks during mathematics classes. Students were given two weeks to solve the problems and prepare for the presentations (with the teacher providing assistance as required).

Students had access to the Internet on two computers in the classroom and during Internet computer time available in the computer room. Some students had access to the Internet through computers at home.

Word Problems For Kids

Made Possible With Funding From:

Canada's SchoolNet   Rescol Canadien

This site has been turbo charged for viewing with Netscape N

This Web Site contains word problems for students and teachers. The problems are classified into grade levels from Grade 5 to Grade 12. THIS IS NOT A TEST, but a set of carefully selected problems which can help you improve your problem solving skills -if you try to carefully think about how you would solve each problem, and once you have found the solution, you make sure that you understand all parts of the solution. You can try any problem you like and if the problem is a little difficult you can get helpful hints by following the hints link. Complete solutions are available to teachers with e-mail addresses upon request.

This web site has been established with support from Industry Canada and is located at St. Francis Xavier University. Our thanks to the Waterloo Mathematics Foundation for their permission to adapt problems from the Canadian Mathematics Competitions.

Courtesy of P. Wang, St. Francis Xavier University, Nova Scotia

Word Problems For Kids.
http://www.stfx.ca/special/mathproblems/welcome.html

Word Problems for Kids is partially interactive in that students can obtain on-line hints and solutions for the problems (the solutions are not as complete as what was expected for the teacher's assignment). The availability of hints was helpful for reducing the amount of time that the teacher spent on assisting students with the assignment.

The teacher was not concerned by the availability of solutions. The stronger students had amply demonstrated that they were able to take ownership of their own learning, and therefore were unlikely to look at the answer without working for a reasonable time on solving the problem. The fact that each pair of students had to present the solutions to their peers in an understandable way and that the grade for the assignment was determined by the effectiveness of the presentation helped to minimize "cheating".

The teacher found this assignment involving the Internet an effective way to have students take a more active role in becoming better problem solvers. The presentations were generally well done and provided students with a good opportunity to increase their problem solving skills.

Example 7: Engaging Students in Communicating

One of the exciting uses of the Internet concerns communication and collaboration with other classrooms. In that regard, the Internet can be an important tool for helping to foster a community of learners that extends well beyond the walls of a single classroom.

Here is one example (Ameis, 1998): A grade 3 teacher was working on data management concepts and skills with her students. Her students collected, graphed, and discussed information on their pets. During the discussion, one student suggested asking students from other classrooms about their pets. That idea soon expanded to using e-mail to collect data on pets from students in other classrooms in the city and beyond. The students were quite excited about this. Because the classroom had a computer connected to the Internet, it was possible to send and receive e-mail in their classroom.

After the students composed a clearly expressed e-mail message (their first task), they determined (with the help of the teacher) where and how to send e-mail messages. Messages were sent to schools in the city and to a few electronic bulletin board services. Several days later, e-mailed information on pets began arriving and arriving and arriving. Information came from as far away as Australia (which created a flurry of interest about Australia).

An entire classroom wall was devoted to recording the information on pets. A new category occasionally had to be included and efficient ways of keeping track of the counts had to be devised. In short, the project on pets was hugely successful. The students worked on it eagerly and had a rich data management learning experience.

Example 8: Engaging Students in Projects

One form of communication and collaboration involves students doing and sharing projects. The Internet offers teachers and students opportunities for stimulating, engaging in, and sharing interesting projects.

One site to visit is **Kids Did This in Math!** (**http://sln.fi.edu/tfi/hotlists/ kid-math.html**). It provides links to sites that promote the sharing of student projects. These links concern a variety of mathematical topics and grade levels. Three examples of the sites that can be accessed (at the time of writing this book) from **Kids Did This in Math!** follow.

Tesselations (http://www.fcps.k12.va.us/ChurchillRoadES/art/artnov56.htm) provides stunning graphics and interesting information on the tesselations involved in Escher's art. For their project, fifth and sixth graders studied the work of M.C. Escher. They experimented with their own designs, creating design patterns that tesselate up and down, left and right and ones that spin as they are repeated. The project involved students doing some worthwhile mathematical thinking in the domain of geometry.

Fifth Grade Math Story Problems (http://www.stignatius.org/5math.htm) provides math story problems that fifth grade students created by using Kid Pix Studio. The problems for the project involved fractions and included illustrations. Such a project creates interest in solving mathematical problems that involve fractions and arithmetic operations.

Ancient Civilizations and their Number Systems (http://www.best.com/~swanson/ancient_numbers/maths_menu.html) involves a joint social studies and mathematics project. Students researched the number systems of the ancient Egyptians, Babylonians, Greeks, Romans, Chinese, Arabs, and Hindus. As well as these compulsory number systems, some students chose to research origins of their own number systems and many of them also chose to look at the Mayan system as the Maya is a topic studied during social studies later in the year. The students then created their own number systems, showing symbols up to 1,000,000 and explained the advantages and disadvantages of their systems. Five student projects are provided on the site.

CHAPTER SUMMARY

The Internet has a role to play in the reform of mathematics education. This chapter provides some reasons why reform is needed and some examples of what can happen when the Internet is used as an instructional tool. These examples are consistent with *Principles and Standards for School Mathematics* (NCTM, 2000).

References

Ameis, J. A. (1998). Data from a study of practicing teachers enrolled in a graduate course that concerned engaging students in mathematical problem solving.

Ameis J. A. (1997). Data from a study of certification year preservice teachers enrolled in a general elementary (K-6) mathematics curriculum and instruction course.

Martinez, J. R. & Martinez, N. C. (1998). In defense of mathematics reform and the NCTM's *Standards. Mathematics Teacher, 91*(9), 746-748.

National Council of Teachers of Mathematics. (2000). *Principles and Standards for School Mathematics.* Reston, VA: Author.

National Council of Teachers of Mathematics. (1989). *Curriculum and Evaluation Standards for School Mathematics.* Reston, VA.: Author.

National Research Council. (1989). *Everybody counts: A report to the nation on the future of mathematics education.* Washington, DC: National Academy Press.

CHAPTER 3

Links to Mathematics Teaching Resources

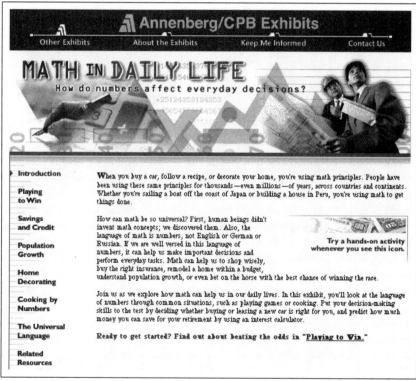

Courtesy of Annenberg/CPB

Math in Daily Life
http://www.learner.org/exhibits/
dailymath/

■ Introduction
■ Lessons and Activities

■ Problems
■ Mathematics Content
■ Statistics
■ Comprehensive Gateways
■ Other Math-related Matters

INTRODUCTION

This chapter is an annotated collection of websites that provide a variety of resources for teaching mathematics. Our intent is to offer a broad sampling of the many Internet sites that contain resources for teaching mathematics. An estimate of the number of such sites is 200,000. Not all are of equal quality, and various criteria are used for determining the quality of a website. For further information on evaluating websites, see the following site, which also provides links to similar sites.

The ABC's of Web Site Evaluation
http://kathyschrock.net/abceval/index.htm

The sites included in this chapter are consistent with the NCTM document *Principles and Standards for School Mathematics*. Additional criteria have also been applied to selecting websites:

■ The links seem reliable.

■ The material at the site is organized in a reasonably pleasing and functional way.

■ The textual material conforms to acceptable standards of grammar, spelling, and clarity of expression.

The sites are organized into six categories: Lessons and Activities; Problems; Mathematics Content; Statistics; Comprehensive Gateways; and Other Math-related Matters. While there is usually some overlap of categories, each site is listed only in the category that best fits the resources the site contains.

Within each category, the sites are organized by grade level zones. The judgement on the grade level suitability of a site's resources is best seen as an approximate guide since the resources often can be applied to a number of grade levels, and because while the authors of the sites sometimes state the intended grade level, more often they do not. Additionally, the grade level suitability of concepts and skills included in curriculum documents is determined largely by state and provincial education authorities and on that there is no universal agreement. Also, the readiness to learn of students must be taken into account when determining grade level suitability.

Useful information provided for each listed site includes its title and URL, a description of its pertinent features, and a profile consisting of eight components. These are:

1. *Intended Audience* refers to the audience (teachers, students, or both) that would benefit most from the material found at the site.

2. *Grade Level* refers to the recommended grade level or levels for the material found at the site.

3. *Curricular Fit* refers to the main mathematics areas/topics that the site addresses (e.g., number concepts, arithmetic algorithms, geometric shapes).

4. *Type of Resources* refers to whether the site is a collection of links to other sites (a gateway site), or a storehouse of specific content (e.g., activities, problems, mathematical ideas), or both.

5. *Authorship of Site* refers to the creator of the site (whether a commercial enterprise, a university/school, government agency, professional organization, or private individual).

6. *Navigation* refers to how simple and convenient it is for the user to access various parts of the site (satisfactory, good, very good).

7. *Visual Appeal* refers to how well the site might capture the user's interest and the extent to which graphics and special effects are used (satisfactory, good, very good). Visual appeal likely has more relevance for sites intended for students. It also provides a rough measure of the site's display speed because a site with very good visual appeal tends to have graphics-rich web pages, which have a slower display speed than pages with minimal graphics.

8. *Interactive Activity* refers to the extent of interaction that is possible between the user and the site's resources (none/minimal, some, extensive). "None" means that the user can only read and look at pictures or go to other links. "Extensive" may mean that the site consists of an interactive game or of a problem or problems for which immediate feedback is provided.

<table>
</table>

Preschool	Fourth	Ninth
Kindergarten	Fifth	Tenth
First	Sixth	Eleventh
Second	Seventh	Twelfth
Third	Eighth	under-graduate

Submit a Lesson

Search the lesson archive for subject, title, grade level, etc.

Send mail to the site manager

Internet Education Resources

Courtesy of William Chapman, University of Illinois

Collaborative Lesson Archive
http://faldo.atmos.uiuc.edu/CLA/

LESSONS AND ACTIVITIES

The following sites contain lessons and/or activities or ideas for creating them. The sites may also include other matters of interest. A few of the sites are gateways (a collection of links) to sites that contain lessons/activities. Most of the sites provide resources specific to grade levels and/or to mathematics curriculum topics.

Elementary to High School Sites

TITLE: **Collaborative Lesson Archive**

http://faldo.atmos.uiuc.edu/CLA/	
Intended Audience	Teachers
Grade Level	K–12 and beyond
Curricular Fit	A variety of curricular topics
Type of Resources	Content and some links
Authorship of Site	University of Illinois (William Chapman)
Navigation	Good
Visual Appeal	Good
Interactive Activity	Some (through submitting lesson plans and commenting on lesson plans used from the database)

Collaborative Lesson Archive is a forum for the creation and distribution of lesson plans for all grade levels and subject areas. Teachers are invited to submit lesson plans and to comment on ones that they have used from the lesson plan archive. Comments about what worked/did not work well in the classroom and about possible improvements are welcomed. This collaboration feature is intended to help refine and refresh lesson plans that are in the archive.

TITLE   **K–12 Lessons Plans**

http://teams.lacoe.edu/documentation/places/lessons.html	
Intended Audience	Teachers
Grade level	K–12
Curricular Fit	A variety of mathematical topics
Type of Resources	Links
Authorship of site	Los Angeles County Office of Education (TEAMS Distance learning)
Navigation	Good
Visual Appeal	Good
Interactive Activity	None

K12 Lessons Plans provides links to a variety of lesson plan sites, including Encarta Mathematics Lessons and Cooperative Learning Lesson Plans.

TITLE: **Mathematics Archives—Teaching Materials**

http://archives.math.utk.edu/teaching.html	
Intended Audience	Teachers
Grade Level	K–12 and beyond
Curricular Fit	A variety of mathematics topics
Type of Resources	Links
Authorship of Site	Mathematics Archives (University of Tennessee)
Navigation	Very good
Visual Appeal	Good
Interactive Activity	None

Mathematics Archives—Teaching Materials is an extensive collection of links to sites that provide teaching resources such as lessons/activities, information on mathematical contests/competitions, and projects and discussion forums concerning graphing calculators. This site is a useful place to begin if you simply want to surf the Net for these resources.

TITLE: **Coolmath.com**

http://www.coolmath.com/home.htm	
Intended Audience	Teachers and students
Grade level	K–12
Curricular Fit	A variety of mathematics topics
Type of resources	Content
Authorship of Site	Coolmath.com, Inc.
Navigation	Very good
Visual Appeal	Very good
Interactive Activity	Some (when playing games and for some activities)

Coolmath.com provides varied resources, including lessons, thinking games, a message board service, and puzzles and problems. It also includes information for students on how to succeed in mathematics and information and links to careers involving mathematics.

TITLE: **Mathematics Projects**

http://www.eduplace.com/projects/mathproj.html	
Intended Audience	Teachers and students
Grade Level	K–12
Curricular Fit	A variety of mathematical topics
Type of Resources	Content and links
Authorship of Site	Houghton Mifflin
Navigation	Very good
Visual Appeal	Good
Interactive Activity	Some (when sharing project information)

Mathematics Projects provides classrooms with an opportunity to submit mathematics projects to it and to participate in projects from other classrooms. The site offers good possibilities for collaborating with other classrooms and teachers.

TITLE: **CEC Lesson Plans**

http://www.col-ed.org/cur/	
Intended Audience	Teachers
Grade Level	K–12
Curricular Fit	A variety of mathematical topics
Type of Resources	Content and links
Authorship of Site	Columbia Education Center, an educational service organization based in Portland, OR
Navigation	Very good
Visual Appeal	Satisfactory
Interactive Activity	Minimal (through providing lesson plans to the site)

CEC Lesson Plans is an extensive collection of lessons in social studies, science, mathematics, language arts, and in a "miscellaneous" category. The mathematics lessons are well organized and provide information on implementation and intended outcomes. Classroom teachers contributed the lessons.

TITLE: **A Tour of Fractions**

http://forum.swarthmore.edu/paths/fractions/	
Intended Audience	Teachers and students
Grade Level	K–12
Curricular Fit	Fractions
Type of Resources	Links and content
Authorship of Site	Swarthmore College
Navigation	Good
Visual Appeal	Good
Interactive Activity	None

A Tour of Fractions provides an extensive collection of links (and some content) to sites that provide lesson/activities for teaching fractions. The resources are categorized into elementary school, middle school, and high school. In addition, resources are provided for students (notably, an archive of other students' questions about fractions that were answered by Dr. Math).

TITLE: **Mathematics Lesson Plans**

http://www.col-ed.org/cur/math.html	
Intended Audience	Teachers
Grade Level	K–12
Curricular Fit	A variety of mathematics topics
Type of Resources	Content
Authorship of Site	Columbia Education Center
Navigation	Satisfactory
Visual Appeal	Satisfactory
Interactive Activity	None

Mathematics Lesson Plans provides a collection of lessons designed by teachers, including information on outcomes, implementation strategies, and extension activities.

TITLE: **SMILE PROGRAM MATHEMATICS INDEX**

http://www.iit.edu/~smile/mathinde.html	
Intended Audience	Teachers
Grade Level	Elementary to high school
Curricular Fit	A variety of mathematics topics
Type of Resources	Content
Authorship of Site	Illinois Institute of Technology, SMILE Program
Navigation	Good
Visual Appeal	Good
Interactive Activity	None

SMILE PROGRAM MATHEMATICS INDEX is a collection of over 200 single concept lessons that are divided into the categories of Geometry and Measurement, Patterns and Logic, Probability and Statistics, Recreational and Creative Math, Practical and Applied Math, Arithmetic, Graphs and Visuals, Algebra and Trigonometry, and Miscellaneous. The lessons were created by teachers who participated in the summer session of the Science and Mathematics Initiative for Learning Enhancement (SMILE) program.

TITLE: **TEACHERS HELPING TEACHERS (math lessons)**

http://www.pacificnet.net/~mandel/Math.html	
Intended Audience	Teachers
Grade Level	K–12
Curricular Fit	A variety of mathematics topics
Type of Resources	Content
Authorship of Site	Teachers Helping Teachers organization (Dr. Scott Mandel, Director)
Navigation	Good
Visual Appeal	Good
Interactive Activity	Minimal (via e-mail when asking for further information about a lesson)

TEACHERS HELPING TEACHERS (math lessons) contains a wide range of lessons that were contributed by teachers from the United States and other countries. The material is updated weekly during the school year. Lessons normally include the e-mail address of the contributing teacher which makes it possible to obtain additional information about a lesson.

TITLE: **Math Activities for K–12 Teachers**

http://daniel.aero.calpoly.edu/~dfrc/Robin/	
Intended Audience	Teachers
Grade Level	K–12
Curricular Fit	A variety of topics
Type of Resources	Content and links
Authorship of Site	California Polytechnic State University
Navigation	Good
Visual Appeal	Satisfactory
Interactive Activity	None

Math Activities for K–12 Teachers provides a collection of mathematics lessons that relate to NASA projects. For example, there is a K–4 lesson, Geometry and Shapes in the X-36, that involves searching for and identifying different geometric shapes in the X-36 aircraft. Information on outcomes and related NCTM standards is provided for the lessons.

TITLE: **Hotlists: Kids Did This!**

http://sln.fi.edu/tfi/hotlists/kid-math.html	
Intended Audience	Students and teachers
Grade Level	Elementary to high school
Curricular Fit	A variety of mathematics topics
Type of Resources	Links
Authorship of Site	Franklin Institute
Navigation	Good
Visual Appeal	Satisfactory
Interactive Activity	Some (when communicating via e-mail)

Hotlists: Kids Did This! provides links to mathematics projects that students in other schools around the world have placed on the Internet. For example, there is a link to a grade 5 project studying which month has the most birthdays, that involves rich graphics and text.

TITLE: **1999 Toshiba/NSTA Laptop Learning Challenge**

http://www.nsta.org/programs/laptop/	
Intended Audience	Teachers
Grade Level	K–12
Curricular Fit	A variety of topics
Type of Resources	Content
Authorship of Site	National Science Teachers Association (NSTA)
Navigation	Good
Visual Appeal	Good
Interactive Activity	None

1999 Toshiba/NSTA Laptop Learning Challenge contains 20 innovative lessons, available as pdf files, that incorporate science, mathematics, and technology. For example, it offers a middle years lesson, "Solar Car Races", that investigates solar energy and the mathematical relationship between the speed of a car and the number of batteries powering it.

TITLE: **PBS TeacherSource: Math**

http://www.pbs.org/teachersource/math.htm	
Intended Audience	Teachers and students
Grade Level	K–12
Curricular Fit	A variety of topics
Type of Resources	Content and some links
Authorship of Site	PBS
Navigation	Good
Visual Appeal	Good
Interactive Activity	Some

PBS TeacherSource: Math offers lesson plans, activities, and information for teachers, as well as on-line activities for students. The lessons and activities are correlated with national and state curriculum standards.

TITLE: **Discovery School's Webmath**

http://school.discovery.com/homeworkhelp/webmath/	
Intended Audience	Students
Grade Level	Elementary to post-secondary
Curricular Fit	A variety of topics
Type of Resources	Content
Authorship of Site	Discovery.com
Navigation	Good
Visual Appeal	Good
Interactive Activity	Extensive

Discovery School's Webmath offers interactive activities that help develop mathematical skills, including long division, converting to and from scientific notation, graphing, and the chain rule in calculus.

Elementary Grades Sites

TITLE: **Willoughby Wanderings**

http://schoolcentral.com/willoughby/default.htm	
Intended Audience	Students and teachers
Grade Level	Elementary grades
Curricular Fit	Arithmetic
Type of Resources	Content
Authorship of Site	Willoughby Elementary School
Navigation	Good
Visual Appeal	Very good
Interactive Activity	Extensive (when doing games, drills, and simulations)

Willoughby Wanderings is a site that students can use directly. It provides an interactive tutorial on the meaning of multiplication as "groups of", drills on multiplication, problem solving that involves addition and subtraction, and a "Donut Shop Manager" simulation.

TITLE: **Math Forum: Ask Dr. Math—Elementary School Level**

http://forum.swarthmore.edu/dr.math/drmath.elem.html	
Intended Audience	Students
Grade Level	K–6
Curricular Fit	A variety of mathematics topics
Type of Resources	Content
Authorship of Site	Swarthmore College
Navigation	Good
Visual Appeal	Satisfactory
Interactive Activity	Extensive (when asking and receiving answers to questions)

    Math Forum: Ask Dr. Math—Elementary School Level lets students ask questions about mathematics and receive answers to their questions. This kind of student inquiry should be encouraged. This site is one of the more popular "ask the expert" sites. The "doctors" who answer students' questions are mathematics educators and mathematicians from around the world. There is an extensive archive of past questions and answers to examine as well. The archive is organized into mathematics topics (for example, subtraction, geometry). This site also includes links to the "Ask Dr. Math" services for middle school and high school.

TITLE: **Academy Curricular Exchange Mathematics Elementary (K–5)**

http://ofcn.org/cyber.serv/academy/ace/math/elem.html	
Intended Audience	Teachers
Grade Level	Primarily K–5
Curricular Fit	A variety of curricular topics
Type of Resources	Content
Authorship of site	Organization for Community Networks, an Ohio non-profit corporation
Navigation	Good
Visual Appeal	Satisfactory
Interactive Activity	Some (through contributing lesson plans)

    Academy Curricular Exchange Mathematics Elementary (K–5) contains a variety of lesson plans that have been contributed by teachers. Some sample lesson plans include: "Ratio: using peanut butter & jelly sandwich (4–6)" and "Exploring base 4 (4)". The site also includes lesson plans for the higher grades.

TITLE: **Eleven Times**

http://www.LearningKingdom.com/eleven/	
Intended Audience	Students and teachers
Grade Level	Elementary grades
Curricular Fit	Multiplication
Type of Resources	Content
Authorship of Site	The Learning Kingdom
Navigation	Very good
Visual Appeal	Very good
Interactive Activity	Some (when doing the Eleven Times Challenge!)

Eleven Times provides information on a shortcut for multiplying by eleven in the form of a tutorial. First, students learn how to use the shortcut. Then they can test their skill and speed using the Eleven Times Challenge! They also can examine why the short cut works, which can motivate students to think about why arithmetic procedures work.

TITLE: **CanTeach: math**

http://www.track0.com/canteach/elementary/math.html	
Intended Audience	Teachers
Grade Level	K–6
Curricular Fit	A variety of mathematics topics
Type of Resources	Content and Links
Authorship of Site	Iram Khan, James Hörner
Navigation	Very good
Visual Appeal	Good
Interactive Activity	None

CanTeach: math provides an extensive collection of lesson plans for teaching arithmetic, patterns and relations, statistics and probability, and geometry and measurement. it also includes ideas for mathematics learning centers.

TITLE: **Fraction Shapes**

http://math.rice.edu/~lanius/Patterns/	
Intended Audience	Teachers and students
Grade Level	About 3–6 (but also useful in later grades)
Curricular Fit	Fraction concepts (e.g., equivalence)
Type of Resources	Content
Authorship of Site	Rice University, TX (Cynthia Lanius)
Navigation	Good
Visual Appeal	Good
Interactive Activity	Some (when requesting solutions)

Fraction Shapes provides Internet-based activities on fraction concepts and adding/subtracting fractions. Answers to questions are available upon request. The activities are designed to stimulate thinking about fractions; they do not encourage the learning of algorithmic procedures (Step 1, Step 2, etc.). Students investigate various geometric shapes to discover relationships between them that can be described in terms of fractions. Students can work independently or with guidance from the teacher.

TITLE: **Teachers' Lab: Patterns in Mathematics**

http://www.learner.org/teacherslab/math/patterns/index.html	
Intended Audience	Students and teachers
Grade Level	Elementary grades
Curricular Fit	Patterns
Type of Resources	Content
Authorship of Site	Annenberg/CPB
Navigation	Good
Visual Appeal	Good
Interactive Activity	Extensive

Teachers' Lab: Patterns in Mathematics provides information for teachers about patterns and three types of interactive activities for students: logic patterns, number patterns, and word patterns. For example, the site offers an interactive activity where the computer makes up a mystery operation and the student figures out what the operation is by looking for a number pattern. The student can alter the numbers the computer uses.

TITLE: **trol = teacher resources on line = trol Index to Games Materials**

http://www.ex.ac.uk/cimt/res2/res2indx.htm	
Intended Audience	Teachers
Grade Level	1–6
Curricular Fit	A variety of mathematics topics, including problem solving
Type of Resources	Content (mostly pdf files) and links
Authorship of Site	Centre for Innovation in Mathematics Teaching, University of Exeter
Navigation	Good
Visual Appeal	Good
Interactive Activity	None

trol = teacher resources on line = trol Index to Games Materials contains useful information on using mathematical games in the classroom to develop skills and to motivate students. This site contains a variety of two-player games such as "put in" and "take out" games and card games. These two-player games are of a type that could well be played, for example, by choice during learning center or playtime. It also has a link to notes for teachers that provides information on other activities for teaching mathematics.

TITLE: **Mardi Gras Math**

http://www.mardigrasday.com/math/	
Intended Audience	Students
Grade Level	Elementary grades
Curricular Fit	Arithmetic
Type of Resources	Content
Authorship of Site	City of New Orleans
Navigation	Good
Visual Appeal	Very good
Interactive Activity	Extensive (when playing the Mardi Gras game)

Mardi Gras Math offers students a motivating way to brush up on their addition and multiplication skills (and order of operations). The original Mardi Gras Math game was designed by a New Orleans third-grade student and used a deck of cards. The electronic form is an updated version of that game.

TITLE: **Tantalizing Tesselations!!**

http://mathcentral.uregina.ca/RR/database/RR.09.96/archamb1.html	
Intended Audience	Teachers
Grade Level	5 (but could be used in grades 4–6)
Curricular Fit	Tesselations and symmetry (flips, slides, and turns)
Type of Resources	Content and links
Authorship of Site	University of Regina, Math Central
Navigation	Satisfactory
Visual Appeal	Very good
Interactive Activity	None

Tantalizing Tesselations!! contains extensive teaching resources for tessela-tions, including a unit on tesselations that integrates language arts and art educa-tion, a list of print resources on tesselations, and links to other sites that involve tesselations. Ten in-depth lesson plans are provided. This is a good site to examine when searching for activities and ideas for teaching tesselations.

TITLE: **The Virtual Abacus**

http://tiger.coe.missouri.edu/software/software.html	
Intended Audience	Students and teachers
Grade Level	Elementary grades
Curricular Fit	Number concepts
Type of Resources	Content
Authorship of Site	College of Education, University of Missouri
Navigation	Good
Visual Appeal	Good
Interactive Activity	Extensive (when using the Virtual Abacus software)

The Virtual Abacus is an interactive, multimedia software tool to help facili-tate number sense and counting skills in children ages six and up. Tje virtual aba-cus is a computer simulation based on the Chinese abacus. It presents exercises on place value, counting, assing, and subtracting. The exercises are organized into four related modules that build upon the skills and understanding learned in the previous module. Visual and audio feedback is provided to the user after ad answer has been submitted. The software can be downloaded from the site.

TITLE: **Mathematics: Web-linked Activities and Lessons**

http://www.mmhschool.com/teach/math/math1.html	
Intended Audience	Teachers
Grade Level	K–6
Curricular Fit	A variety of mathematics topics
Type of Resources	Links and content
Authorship of Site	Commercial (McGraw-Hill)
Navigation	Very good
Visual Appeal	Good
Interactive Activity	Some (when using CyberScout to locate websites)

Mathematics: Web-linked Activities and Lessons is a collection of links to other mathematics sites and to content from McGraw-Hill's programs *Math in My World* and *Math for You and Me!* This site features CyberScout, a search engine that allows a teacher to search for websites that match his or her mathematics curriculum.

Elementary Grades and Middle Years Sites

TITLE: **PIGS Space: Cooperative Learning—Modules**

http://cspace.unb.ca/nbco/pigs/modules/	
Intended Audience	Teachers
Grade Level	K–8
Curricular Fit	A variety of curricular topics
Type of Resources	Content
Authorship of Site	New Brunswick School Districts
Navigation	Very good
Visual Appeal	Satisfactory
Interactive Activity	Some (through contributing lesson plans)

PIGS Space: Cooperative Learning—Modules focuses on cooperative learning in language arts, mathematics, science, and social studies. The site contains lesson plans developed by New Brunswick teachers. Each lesson plan is directly related to the New Brunswick Curriculum but the lesson plans can be easily adapted to other curricula. Suggestions for enrichment activities often are included. The site's home page also provides links to websites that contain cooperative learning resources and student projects.

TITLE: **Welcome to Wonderful Ideas**

http://www.wonderful.com/	
Intended Audience	Teachers and students
Grade Level	3–8
Curricular Fit	Activities and problems
Type of Resources	Content
Authorship of Site	The Institute for Math Mania
Navigation	Good
Visual Appeal	Good
Interactive Activity	Minimal (when contributing ideas)

Welcome to Wonderful Ideas offers activities and games for teachers to use and problems for students to solve. For example, the site also offers a math contest.

TITLE: **Flash Cards for Kids!**

http://www.edu4kids.com/math/	
Intended Audience	Students
Grade Level	4–8
Curricular Fit	Arithmetic
Type of Resources	Content
Authorship of Site	Flashcards for Kids
Navigation	Very good
Visual Appeal	Satisfactory
Interactive Activity	Extensive (when doing the exercises)

Flash Cards for Kids! offers students practice on basic arithmetic facts and more. Students set the conditions for the practice (the arithmetic operation, the type and number of numbers, the size of the numbers) and then the site provides a series of single questions for students to answer. Feedback is provided on each question.

TITLE: **Harcourt Multimedia Math Glossary**

http://www.harcourtschool.com/glossary/math/index.html	
Intended Audience	Students
Grade Level	K–8
Curricular Fit	A variety of mathematical topics
Type of Resources	Content
Authorship of site	Harcourt School Publishers
Navigation	Very good
Visual Appeal	Very good
Interactive Activity	Some (through selecting and watching animated definitions of terms)

Harcourt Multimedia Math Glossary provides definitions of mathematical terms students may encounter from grade 1 to grade 8. Most definitions are animated to explain concepts in a visual and informative way. Students will enjoy using this reference tool to learn mathematics terminology.

TITLE: **Mathematics Activities Guides**

http://cesme.utm.edu/resources/math/MAG/Mag.html	
Intended Audience	Teachers
Grade Level	K–8
Curricular Fit	A variety of mathematics topics
Type of Resources	Content
Authorship of Site	University of Tennessee at Martin
Navigation	Very good
Visual Appeal	Good
Interactive Activity	None

Mathematics Activities Guides contains a large collection of lessons organized into K–2, 3–5, and 6–8 levels. Each level has five lesson categories: Number Sense and Theory; Estimation, Measurement, and Computation; Patterns, Functions, and Algebraic Thinking; Statistics and Probability; Spatial Sense and Geometric Concepts. The lessons are stored as PDF files, which means that Acrobat Reader is required for accessing the lessons (Acrobat Reader can be downloaded from the site).

TITLE: **Funbrain**

http://www.funbrain.com	
Intended Audience	Teachers and students
Grade Level	Elementary and middle years
Curricular Fit	A variety of topics
Type of Resources	Content
Authorship of Site	Learning Network, 2000
Navigation	Good
Visual Appeal	Satisfactory
Interactive Activity	Extensive

Funbrain contains interactive games and exercises for students. For example, it offers an interactive place value and rounding activity. This site also has resources for teachers, including a feature that allows teachers to create quizzes on-line.

TITLE: **LessonPlansPage.com!**

http://www.lessonplanspage.com/Math.htm	
Intended Audience	Teachers
Grade Level	Primarily 1–8
Curricular Fit	A variety of mathematics topics
Type of Resources	Content
Authorship of Site	EdScope, L.L.C.
Navigation	Good
Visual Appeal	Good
Interactive Activity	Some (when providing feedback on or contributing lessons)

LessonPlansPage.com is a collection of hundreds of lessons. Some examples are a math lesson on subtraction using area codes distance for grades 4 and 5, a math lesson on measuring distance for grades 6 and 7, a math lesson that involves writing fairy tales for grades 2 and 3, and a math lesson on two-dimensional shapes for grades K and 1.

Middle Years Sites

TITLE: **Math Projects for Science Fairs**

http://camel.math.ca/Education/mpsf/	
Intended Audience	Teachers
Grade Level	5–9
Curricular Fit	A variety of mathematics topics
Type of Resources	Content
Authorship of Site	Canadian Mathematical Society
Navigation	Good
Visual Appeal	Satisfactory
Interactive Activity	None

Math Projects for Science Fairs provides a wealth of ideas that can be used in the classroom as well as for mathematics projects that can be entered in science fairs. Some of the ideas are more interesting than others, some require more mathematics background than others, and some have more room for exploration than others. The site also provides guidance on what a mathematics project might look like.

TITLE: **Centre for Innovation in Mathematics Teaching—Bar Codes**

http://www.ex.ac.uk/cimt/resource/barcode.htm	
Intended Audience	Teachers and students
Grade Level	Middle years
Curricular Fit	Number concepts
Type of Resources	Content
Authorship of Site	University of Exeter
Navigation	Good
Visual Appeal	Very good
Interactive Activity	None

Centre for Innovation in Mathematics Teaching—Bar Codes provides clear information on bar codes and related questions for students to work on. The site's home page offers other interesting resources that concern real-world applications of mathematics (for example, genetic fingerprinting, posting parcels) and that concern other curricular matters (for example, puzzles and computer programs).

Middle Years and High School Sites

TITLE: **ALGEBRA**

http://forum.swarthmore.edu/sum95/sinclair/alg1.html	
Intended Audience	Teachers
Grade Level	7–12
Curricular Fit	Algebra
Type of Resources	Content and links
Authorship of Site	Math Forum
Navigation	Good
Visual Appeal	Good
Interactive Activity	None

ALGEBRA offers algebra lessons and activities and provides links to computer resources for teaching algebra, to applications and history of algebra, and to possible careers involving mathematics. It is a good place to begin when searching for useful ideas to teach algebra.

TITLE: **Applied Academics**

http://www.bced.gov.bc.ca/careers/aa/	
Intended Audience	Students and teachers
Grade Level	Middle years and up
Curricular Fit	A variety of topics
Type of Resources	Content
Authorship of Site	British Columbia Ministry of Education
Navigation	Good
Visual Appeal	Satisfactory
Interactive Activity	None

Applied Academics offers a collection of lesson plans that link mathematics to specific occupations. The lessons help students understand how different professions use mathematics.

TITLE: **Lessons to Motivate Underachieving Math Students**

http://www.mste.uiuc.edu/mccall/mainlesson.html	
Intended Audience	Teachers
Grade Level	8–12
Curricular Fit	A variety of mathematics topics
Type of Resources	Links
Authorship of Site	University of Illinois at Urbana-Champaign
Navigation	Good
Visual Appeal	Satisfactory
Interactive Activity	None

Lessons to Motivate Underachieving Math Students is a gateway site that provides a collection of links to sites that contain a variety of lessons/activities that are useful for motivating students who underachieve in mathematics. The major categories of the links provided are: (1) math lessons by topics of interest to students, (2) math lessons using websites, (3) math lessons using spreadsheets, (4) math lessons using hypercard stacks, (5) math lessons using mathematical models, and (6) math lessons created by students. This site also contains links to other kinds of sites (for example, PUMP Algebra Curriculum).

TITLE: **Tools for Understanding**

http://www.ups.edu/community/tofu/	
Intended Audience	Teachers
Grade Level	Middle years and high school
Curricular Fit	A variety of topics related to using a spreadsheet or calculator
Type of Resources	Content
Authorship of Site	University of Puget Sound (John Woodward)
Navigation	Good
Visual Appeal	Satisfactory
Interactive Activity	None

Tools for Understanding provides mathematics lessons that use a spreadsheet or a calculator to help teach mathematics and basic lessons on using a spreadsheet. The mathematics lessons include working with fractions, finding area and perimeter, and analyzing data. This site is helpful for teachers who want to integrate common technologies into mathematics instruction.

TITLE: **A Web-based Interactive Stock Market Learning Project for K–12**

http://www.ncsa.uiuc.edu/edu/rse/RSEyellow/gnb.html	
Intended Audience	Teachers and students
Grade Level	Middle Years and up
Curricular Fit	Consumer mathematics, statistics, probability
Type of Resources	Content and links
Authorship of Site	University of Illinois at Urbana-Champaign, Resource for Science Education Program (RSE)
Navigation	Good
Visual Appeal	Good
Interactive Activity	Some (when gathering stock market data)

A Web-based Interactive Stock Market Learning Project for K–12 presents an interdisciplinary project designed for middle school students and teachers that revolves around an interactive stock market competition between classmates using real-time stock market data from the New York Stock Exchange and NASDAQ. The site includes lessons and other material from a variety of subject areas. The lessons and warm-up discussion topics give students an understanding of how the stock market works and how it is an integral part of daily life.

TITLE: **Self-Similarity**

http://math.rice.edu/~lanius/fractals/self.html	
Intended Audience	Students and teachers
Grade Level	Lower middle years and up
Curricular Fit	Geometry (similarity and fractals)
Type of Resources	Content and links
Authorship of Site	Rice University (Cynthia Lanius)
Navigation	Good
Visual Appeal	Good
Interactive Activity	Some (when following directions)

Self-Similarity provides students with a set of activities that are intended to help them understand self-similarity and fractals. The activities are student-friendly and motivating (for example, making a Jurassic Park fractal) and have clear instructions. The site also provides teacher notes and links to related sites.

TITLE: **MAT 476—Teaching Mathematics in the Middle and Secondary Schools**

http://euclid.barry.edu/~marinas/mat476/lessons.html	
Intended Audience	Teachers
Grade Level	Middle years and up
Curricular Fit	A variety of mathematics topics (integrated with other matters)
Type of Resources	Content
Authorship of Site	Barry University, FL (Carol Marinas)
Navigation	Good
Visual Appeal	Good
Interactive Activity	None

MAT 476—TEACHING MATHEMATICS IN THE MIDDLE AND SECOND-ARY SCHOOLS is a collection of rich lesson plans that often integrate mathematics with other matters (e.g., a problem situated in the context of visiting the Metro Zoo in Miami). The lessons are specific to south Florida but they easily can be modified to suit other geographical locations. The lessons include information on outcomes and on how the lessons reflect one or more of the NCTM *Standards*.

High School Sites

TITLE: **High School Math Project Ideas**

http://www.columbia.edu/~umk1/#MATHSITES	
Intended Audience	Teachers
Grade Level	High school
Curricular Fit	Probability and algebra
Type of Resources	Content and links
Authorship of Site	Coalition School for Social Change
Navigation	Very good
Visual Appeal	Good
Interactive Activity	Some (when contributing projects)

High School Math Project Ideas contains some high school mathematics projects (e.g., probability: genetics). Detailed information is provided on each project, including intended outcomes, rubrics for assessment, and prerequisite knowledge. Contributions of projects are welcome.

TITLE: **Exercises in Math Readiness for University Study**

http://math.usask.ca/readin/index.html	
Intended Audience	Students and teachers
Grade Level	High school
Curricular Fit	A variety of mathematics topics
Type of Resources	Content
Authorship of Site	University of Saskatchewan
Navigation	Good
Visual Appeal	Good
Interactive Activity	Extensive (when doing questions and requesting answers)

Exercises in Math Readiness for University Study consists of exercises on those high school mathematics topics that seem to be most important for university study in mathematics, the other sciences, engineering, and commerce. Students select a topic (for example, trigonometric functions, modeling real world problems, graphing polynomials) and the site presents questions on the topic for students to answer. Upon request, they can view detailed answers to the questions.

TITLE: **Browse MathSource**

http://www.mathsource.com/	
Intended Audience	Teachers and students
Grade Level	High school
Curricular Fit	A variety of mathematics topics
Type of Resources	Content
Authorship of Site	Wolfram Research Inc.—makers of *Mathematica*
Navigation	Good
Visual Appeal	Very good
Interactive Activity	Some

Browse MathSource is a vast electronic library of *Mathematica* materials (e.g., *Mathematica* programs, documents) that are immediately accessible. Browse the archive or search by author, title, keyword, or item number. The site welcomes contributions of *Mathematica* material.

TITLE: **Conjectures in Geometry**

http://www.geom.umn.edu/~dwiggins/mainpage.html	
Intended Audience	Students and teachers
Grade Level	High school
Curricular Fit	Geometry
Type of Resources	Content
Authorship of Site	University of Minnesota (Jodi Crane, Linda Stevens, and Dave Wiggins)
Navigation	Good
Visual Appeal	Good
Interactive Activity	Extensive (when using Sketch Pad)

Conjectures in Geometry contains 20 geometry conjectures to be investigated by students using Sketch Pad. It can be downloaded from the site. Some examples of the conjectures are polygon sum conjecture (sum of the angles for any convex polygon), midsegment conjectures (lengths of midsegments for triangles and trapezoids), rhombus conjectures (side, angle, and diagonal relationships).

TITLE: **Geometry Online**

http://math.rice.edu/~lanius/Geom/	
Intended Audience	Teachers and students
Grade Level	High school
Curricular Fit	Geometry
Type of Resources	Content and some links
Authorship of Site	Rice University (Cynthia Lanius)
Navigation	Good
Visual Appeal	Good
Interactive Activity	Some (answering questions via e-mail)

Geometry Online contains geometry activities suitable for high school. Two sample activities are "Isosceles Triangle Puzzler" and "Circles around Pythagoras". Some of the activities are interactive in that students can e-mail responses to questions that are part of the activity and then receive feedback. A new activity is added to the list roughly once a month.

TITLE: **High School Learning Units**

http://www.nsa.gov/programs/mepp/hs.html	
Intended Audience	Teachers
Grade Level	High school
Curricular Fit	A variety of mathematical topics
Type of Resources	Content
Authorship of Site	Mathematics Education Partnership Program (MEPP)
Navigation	Good
Visual Appeal	Satisfactory
Interactive Activity	None

High School Learning Units provides a collection of learning units on pre-algebra, algebra, geometry, trigonometry, statistics, pre-calculus, and calculus. Information on how the lessons relate to the NCTM *Standards* is included, along with worksheets that can be downloaded.

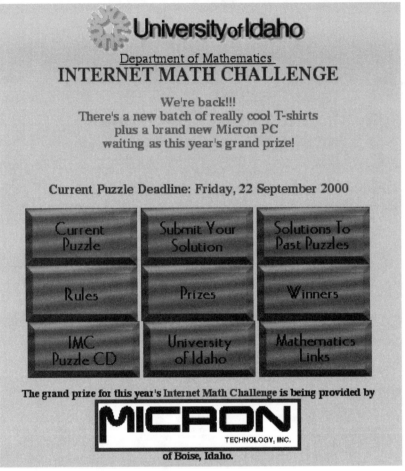

Courtesy of University of Idaho Mathematics Department

University of Idaho INTERNET MATH CHALLENGE
http://www.uidaho.edu/LS/math/imc/

PROBLEMS

The following sites concern problem solving but may also address other matters of interest. Some sites contain specific kinds of problems while others contain a variety. Some sites involve extensive interactivity; most have limited or no interactivity.

Elementary to High School Sites

TITLE: **MATH**

http://www.nhusd.k12.ca.us/ALVE/ace/Math/%20Math.html	
Intended Audience	Teachers and students
Grade Level	Elementary grades and up
Curricular Fit	Problem solving
Type of Resources	Links
Authorship of Site	A.C.E. (Alvarado Cyber Explorers)
Navigation	Very good
Visual Appeal	Very good
Interactive Activity	None

MATH is a gateway site that provides links to sites that contain problems. The four categories of links are Brain Teasers, General, Geometry, and Puzzles. Some of the links go to sites that also concern mathematics topics such as topology.

TITLE: **Welcome to the NRICH Online Maths Club**

http://www.nrich.maths.org.uk/	
Intended Audience	Students and teachers
Grade Level	K–12
Curricular Fit	Problem solving
Type of Resources	Content and links
Authorship of Site	University of Cambridge, UK
Navigation	Very good
Visual Appeal	Good
Interactive Activity	Some (via e-mail and solution submissions, and by requesting hints and solutions)

Welcome to the NRICH Online Maths Club is devoted to providing interesting and challenging problems that can be used for enrichment. A bulletin board and magazine service are also available. Students can submit their solutions for publication on the site. This site can be very valuable for facilitating problem solving.

TITLE: **Fermi Questions**

http://forum.swarthmore.edu/workshops/sum96/interdisc/sheila1.html	
Intended Audience	Teachers and students
Grade Level	K–12
Curricular Fit	Problem solving
Type of Resources	Content and links
Authorship of Site	Swarthmore College (Sheila Talamo)
Navigation	Good
Visual Appeal	Good
Interactive Activity	Some (when submitting solutions and contributing problems)

Fermi questions provides information on Fermi problems (what they are and why they are useful in the classroom) and contains a collection of them. Fermi problems emphasize estimation, numerical reasoning, assumption making, and questioning skills (for example, How many fish are there in the ocean?). These kinds of problems encourage multiple approaches and help students understand that problems do not have to have only one correct answer. Teachers and students have the opportunity to submit solutions to the site's Fermi problems and to contribute additional Fermi problems for the library. Selected solutions are posted on-line.

TITLE: **Colourful Mathematics**

http://www.math.ucalgary.ca/~laf/colorful/colorful.html	
Intended Audience	Students and teachers
Grade Level	Elementary and up
Curricular Fit	Problem solving that is related to graph theory
Type of Resources	Content and links to related sites
Authorship of Site	University of Calgary
Navigation	Good
Visual Appeal	Good
Interactive Activity	Some (by downloading game software and using it to work on a problem)

Colourful Mathematics exposes students to five real problems of contemporary mathematics, cast in game format. All five games involve a search for and discovery of patterns, which are at the very heart of mathematics. The games utilize simple coloring and/or drawing techniques to illustrate the mathematical concept underlying the game. The site provides teachers with background information on the problems and software for each game can be downloaded from the site.

TITLE: **This is Mega Mathematics!**

http://www.c3.lanl.gov/mega-math/	
Intended Audience	Teachers and students
Grade Level	3–12
Curricular Fit	Unusual topics such as topology
Type of Resources	Links and content
Authorship of Site	Computer Research and Applications Group of Los Alamos National Laboratory
Navigation	Good
Visual Appeal	Very good
Interactive Activity	Some

This is Mega Mathematics! provides a small collection of interesting problems that students and teachers can access. Additional resources for the problems are available as well in the form of evaluation information, big ideas and key concepts information, vocabulary, stories, background information, and preparation and materials information. The site is well worth visiting for its unusual and stimulating problems.

TITLE: **Brain Teasers**

http://www.eduplace.com/math/brain/	
Intended Audience	Teachers and students
Grade Level	3 and up
Curricular Fit	Problem solving
Type of Resources	Content
Authorship of Site	Houghton Mifflin
Navigation	Good
Visual Appeal	Good
Interactive Activity	Some (when providing answers to the problems and when using the hints option)

Brain Teasers provides an opportunity for students to solve weekly problems and to submit answers to them. The problems involve a variety of mathematical topics (e.g., geometry, number concepts). One problem is presented each week for each of the three grade levels (3–4, 5–6, 7 and up). Hints are available. Solutions are posted the following week. Previous problems and solutions can be accessed through an archive collection.

TITLE: **The All New & Improved Fruit Game**

http://www.2020tech.com/fruit/	
Intended Audience	Students
Grade Level	3 and up
Curricular Fit	Problem solving
Type of Resources	Content
Authorship of Site	Commercial (20/20 Technologies)
Navigation	Very good
Visual Appeal	Very good
Interactive Activity	Extensive (when playing the fruit game)

The All New & Improved Fruit Game is an interesting interactive game site that encourages students to analyze the game for the winning strategy. The site can be used to promote interest in thinking about winning strategies for other unfair games (those that have a winning strategy for the first or the second player). This site is best for students who appreciate challenges and who do not need to always win. It offers a send-a-letter option for those students who wish to provide feedback on the game.

TITLE: **UCF CASIO CONTENT PAGE**

http://pegasus.cc.ucf.edu/~mathed/problem.html	
Intended Audience	Students and teachers (the archives)
Grade Level	3–12
Curricular Fit	Problem solving
Type of Resources	Content
Authorship of Site	University of Mississippi
Navigation	Good
Visual Appeal	Very good
Interactive Activity	Some (when submitting solutions)

UCF CASIO CONTENT PAGE involves a weekly problem solving contest organized into three grade level categories (grade 6 or below, grades 6–8, and grades 6–12) and an open category. Solutions (along with explanations) are submitted via e-mail. The names of students submitting correct solutions are published on the site. For each category of problems, a weekly winner is randomly selected from the pool of correct solutions. The prize is a Casio calculator. Also there is an archive of past problems for each category. This site is useful for finding reasonable problems and for stimulating students to do problem solving.

Elementary Grades Sites

TITLE: **NUMBER and WORD PUZZLES**

http://www1.tpgi.com.au/users/puzzles/	
Intended Audience	Students and teachers
Grade Level	Elementary grades
Curricular Fit	Problem solving (arithmetic, number concepts)
Type of Resources	Content
Authorship of Site	Auspac Media, Australia
Navigation	Good
Visual Appeal	Good
Interactive Activity	Some (over 20 puzzles are interactive)

NUMBER and WORD PUZZLES contains a substantial collection of number puzzles (crossword puzzles that involve numbers rather than words) and other kinds of puzzles (e.g., cryptarithmetic). Some are simple (warm-ups) and others are not (these involve substantial problem solving). Solutions are available on the site. New puzzles appear each month. The puzzles are useful for providing students with needed arithmetic practice in a problem-solving way.

TITLE: **Math for Kids—A Medieval Problem-solving Adventure**

http://tqjunior.advanced.org/4471/Default.htm	
Intended Audience	Students
Grade Level	3–5
Curricular Fit	Problem solving
Type of Resources	Content and links
Authorship of Site	ThinkQuest Jr. Team
Navigation	Good
Visual Appeal	Good
Interactive Activity	Some (through voting for your favorite problem or submitting a word problem)

Math for Kids—A Medieval Problem-solving Adventure was designed by two fourth graders and is intended for students who want to improve their mathematics problem-solving skills. The site provides opportunities for students to practice word problems, to learn how to solve problems, and to share word problems. The problems contained at the site are based on the theme of medieval history and knights.

TITLE: **Mathematical Tale Winds**

http://www.uwinnipeg.ca/~jameis/	
Intended Audience	Teachers and students
Grade Level	3–5
Curricular Fit	Problem solving
Type of Resources	Content
Authorship of Site	University of Winnipeg (Jerry Ameis)
Navigation	Very good
Visual Appeal	Good
Interactive Activity	Minimal (when providing illustrations)

Mathematical Tale Winds offers two types of mathematics problems. There are nonroutine problems embedded in short stories about the adventures of pnomes who live in the land of Pome. There are routine and nonroutine problems embedded in a story, *The Circle of Flame*. This ongoing story has a chapter added to it every couple of months.

Elementary to Middle Years Sites

TITLE: **Mathstories.com**

http://www.mathstories.com/	
Intended Audience	Teachers and students
Grade Level	1–8
Curricular Fit	Problem solving
Type of Resources	Content
Authorship of Site	Mathstories.com
Navigation	Good
Visual Appeal	Good
Interactive Activity	Minimal (when contributing problems)

Mathstories.com provides a collection of over 4,000 math story problems organized by grade level and topic. This site's goal is to help grades 1 to 8 students improve their math problem-solving and critical thinking skills.

TITLE: **Math Maniac's Home Page**

http://www.geocities.com/Athens/Ithaca/2475/mathmaniac.html	
Intended Audience	Students and teachers
Grade Level	Elementary and middle years
Curricular Fit	Problem solving, tesselations
Type of Resources	Content and links
Authorship of Site	Math Maniac
Navigation	Good
Visual Appeal	Good
Interactive Activity	Minimal (when e-mailing solutions to problems)

Math Maniac's Home Page offers weekly problems and solutions, as well as information, including graphics, and links to resources on tesselations.

Middle Years Sites

TITLE: **Mathmania**

http://www.theory.csc.uvic.ca/~mmania/index.html	
Intended Audience	Students and teachers
Grade Level	4–8
Curricular Fit	Geometry (topology)
Type of Resources	Content
Authorship of Site	University of Victoria, BC, Mathmania
Navigation	Good
Visual Appeal	Good
Interactive Activity	Some (when doing tutorials and solving problems)

Mathmania is dedicated to helping students explore topics in topology (sometimes known as rubber sheet geometry). Topology is concerned with investigating properties of shapes and structures that are independent of quantity. For example, a square and a circle (of whatever size) are considered to be the same kind of shape in topology (a square can be turned into a circle and vice versa). The site contains problems along with stories, activities, and other materials to help students work on the problems. Many of the topics involve a hands-on approach. There also is a teacher's section that provides implementation information on integrating the site's resources into the mathematics curriculum.

TITLE: **MATHCOUNTS**

http://206.152.229.6/	
Intended Audience	Students and teachers
Grade Level	7–8
Curricular Fit	Problem solving
Type of Resources	Content
Authorship of Site	MATHCOUNTS Foundation (VA)
Navigation	Good
Visual Appeal	Good
Interactive Activity	Some (via discussions about problem solving)

MATHCOUNTS is a math coaching and competition program that promotes seventh and eighth grade math achievement through grass roots involvement in the United States. MATHCOUNTS is designed to stimulate student interest in math by making math achievement as challenging, exciting, and prestigious as a school sport. Each fall, MATHCOUNTS distributes its free School Handbook and other coaching materials to schools across the country. Teachers and volunteers can use these materials to coach students, either as a part of in-class instruction or as an extracurricular activity. There is an opportunity for students and teachers to participate in discussions about problem solving (via the "Meeting Place" link).

TITLE: **The Little Math Puzzle Contest**

http://www.odyssee.net/~academy/mathpuzzle/	
Intended Audience	Students and teachers
Grade Level	5–9
Curricular Fit	Problem solving with an emphasis on patterns
Type of Resources	Content
Authorship of Site	Royal West Academy High School, Montreal, Quebec
Navigation	Good
Visual Appeal	Satisfactory
Interactive Activity	Some (by submitting a solution to the puzzle of the week)

The Little Math Puzzle Contest offers a math puzzle contest that is open to all participants but is designed for students in grades 5 through 10. A new puzzle is posted each week along with the names of the weekly winners. An explanation for the answer is encouraged but not required. Teachers can obtain solutions by written request for the password.

Middle Years to High School Sites

TITLE: **Word Problems for Kids**

http://www.stfx.ca/special/mathproblems/welcome.html	
Intended Audience	Students and teachers
Grade Level	5–12
Curricular Fit	Problem solving
Type of Resources	Content
Authorship of Site	St. Francis Xavier University, Nova Scotia
Navigation	Good
Visual Appeal	Good
Interactive Activity	Some (when asking for hints)

Word Problems for Kids provides problems that are designed to improve problem-solving skills. Some of the problems have been adapted from Waterloo University's Canadian Mathematics Competitions. Students can access the problems and hints are available by following the hints link.

TITLE: **Interactive Mathematics Miscellany and Puzzles**

http://www.cut-the-knot.com/	
Intended Audience	Students and teachers
Grade Level	Middle years and up
Curricular Fit	Problem solving
Type of Resources	Content
Authorship of Site	Private individual (Alexander Bogomolny)
Navigation	Good
Visual Appeal	Good
Interactive Activity	Extensive (solving interactive puzzles)

Interactive Mathematics Miscellany and Puzzles provides a good collection of interactive puzzles/games for students to solve. These puzzles/games can be used to stimulate investigation into winning strategies and the underlying mathematics. For example, some of the games are variants of Nim where the winning strategy usually involves some application of a number concept (e.g., multiples). The site also has interesting information on mathematics (for example, the origin of the word algorithm, curves that fill a plane).

TITLE: **Math Forum: K–12 Math Problems, Puzzles, Tips & Tricks**

http://forum.swarthmore.edu/k12/mathtips/	
Intended Audience	Students and teachers
Grade Level	5 and up
Curricular Fit	Problem solving
Type of Resources	Content
Authorship of Site	Swarthmore College
Navigation	Good
Visual Appeal	Good
Interactive Activity	Some (when requesting hints/solutions)

Math Forum: K–12 Math Problems, Puzzles, Tips & Tricks provides a variety of problems, include problems from the Russian Math Olympiads, number & line puzzles, and critical thinking problems. Solutions are available.

High School Sites

TITLE: **University of Idaho Mathematics Department Internet Challenge**

http://www.uidaho.edu/LS/math/imc/	
Intended Audience	Students and teachers
Grade Level	Mostly high school
Curricular Fit	Problem solving
Type of Resources	Links and content
Authorship of Site	University of Idaho Mathematics Department
Navigation	Very good
Visual Appeal	Very good
Interactive Activity	Some (via e-mail)

University of Idaho Mathematics Department Internet Challenge presents a weekly problem to solve. Any student or group of students (in grade 12 or lower) attending a U.S. school is eligible to submit a solution (it must include work and reasoning) via e-mail. Names of all those submitting correct solutions are posted on the site. A weekly prize of a T-shirt is given to the person selected at random from the pool of correct solution submissions.

TITLE: **The Grey Labyrinth: Puzzles**

http://www.greylabyrinth.com/puzzles.htm	
Intended Audience	Teachers and students
Grade Level	11–12
Curricular Fit	Problem solving (involving a variety of mathematics topics, including some integration with science)
Type of Resources	Content
Authorship of Site	Commercial (2000 Wx3)
Navigation	Very good
Visual Appeal	Very good
Interactive Activity	Some (via e-mail and a discussion forum)

The Grey Labyrinth: Puzzles is a collection of very challenging, interesting, and unusual problems that are designed to really stimulate thinking. Solutions are provided, but not to all of the problems. This site is for those seeking enrichment problems.

TITLE: **Mudd Math Fun Facts**

http://www.math.hmc.edu/funfacts/	
Intended Audience	Teachers and students
Grade Level	High school and post-secondary
Curricular Fit	A variety of topics
Type of Resources	Content
Authorship of Site	Francis Su
Navigation	Good
Visual Appeal	Satisfactory
Interactive Activity	Minimal (when rating a fun fact and when contributing an item)

Mudd Math Fun Facts provides a collection of mathematics tidbits and challenges that can be used to stimulate problem solving and thinking about mathematics.

TITLE: **Index to Journal and Contest Problems**

http://problems.math.umr.edu/index.htm	
Intended Audience	Teachers
Grade Level	High school and post-secondary
Curricular Fit	A variety of mathematical topics
Type of Resources	Links
Authorship of Site	University of Missouri at Rolla
Navigation	Good
Visual Appeal	Satisfactory
Interactive Activity	Minimal (when searching the database)

Index to Journal and Contest Problems contains a searchable database of links to more than 20,000 challenging mathematics problems from journals and contests.

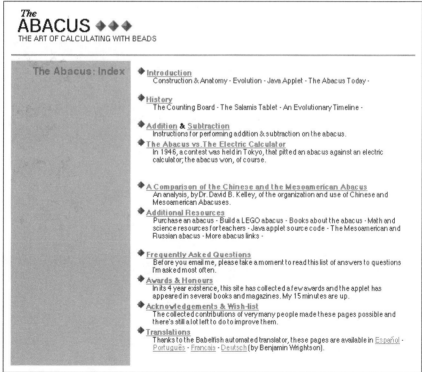

Courtesy of Ryerson Polytechnic University, Department of Electrical and Computer Engineering (Luis Fernandes)

The ABACUS
http://www.ee.ryerson.ca:8080/~elf/abacus/

MATHEMATICS CONTENT

The websites included in this category reflect a variety of mathematical topics (for example, game theory, number theory, Mayan numbers). There is a minor emphasis on mathematics of recent vintage (chaos theory and fractals). The resources found at the sites can be used to stimulate students' inquiry into mathematics and can be used as sources of ideas for designing interesting and motivating classroom activities.

Elementary to High School Sites

TITLE: **The Abacus**

http://www.ee.ryerson.ca:8080/~elf/abacus/	
Intended Audience	Teachers and students
Grade Level	4 and up
Curricular Fit	Arithmetic and number concepts
Type of Resources	Content
Authorship of Site	Ryerson Technical Institute, Ontario
Navigation	Good
Visual Appeal	Good
Interactive Activity	Minimal (some animation is available)

The Abacus is a site that provides information and instruction on using the Chinese abacus to do addition and subtraction. It also provides information on the Japanese and Aztec abacuses and provides links to other abacus sites (including a site for building a LEGO abacus).

TITLE: **About.com: Mathematics**

http://math.about.com/science/math/	
Intended Audience	Teachers
Grade Level	K–12
Curricular Fit	A variety of topics
Type of Resources	Links
Authorship of Site	About.com, Inc.
Navigation	Good
Visual Appeal	Satisfactory
Interactive Activity	None

About.com: Mathematics is a gateway to mathematics information about mathematical concepts. For example, it provides links to number theory and discrete math. It also provides links to lesson plans, activities, and problems.

TITLE: **cryptofr.html**

http://www.achiever.com/freehmpg/cryptology/cryptofr.html	
Intended Audience	Teachers and students
Grade Level	About grade 4/5 and up
Curricular Fit	Number systems (e.g., binary) and transformations (decoding and encoding data), applied mathematics (cryptology)
Type of Resources	Content and links
Authorship of Site	Private individual (Ken Dunham)
Navigation	Very good
Visual Appeal	Good

Cryptofr.html is an excellent site for obtaining information on some of the mathematics involved in encoding and decoding data. It offers comprehensive and extensive information on cryptology (making secret messages and the like). The many cryptology topics contained at the site include information for teachers and students on binary and hexadecimal numbers, bar codes, the history of cryptology, simple ciphers and codes (elementary school level material), Morse code, silent language, and making invisible ink. The site also provides links to other cryptology sites.

TITLE: **The Fibonacci Numbers and the Golden Section**

http://www.mcs.surrey.ac.uk/Personal/R.Knott/Fibonacci/fib.html	
Intended Audience	Teachers and students
Grade Level	Upper elementary grades and up
Curricular Fit	Number theory (Fibonacci numbers, golden section)
Type of Resources	Content and links to other Fibonacci sites
Authorship of Site	Department of Computing, Surrey University, UK
Navigation	Satisfactory
Visual Appeal	Good
Interactive Activity	None

The Fibonacci Numbers and the Golden Section offers a wealth of in-depth information on Fibonacci numbers and related numbers. For example, there is extensive information on Fibonacci numbers in nature and on the history of these numbers. The information found at the site can be used to design interesting student activities. The site also provides some useful activities. This site is recommended for those wanting comprehensive information on the Fibonacci numbers.

TITLE: **Moebius Strip**

http://www.cut-the-knot.com/do_you_know/moebius.html	
Intended Audience	Teachers and students
Grade Level	Elementary grades and up
Curricular Fit	Geometry (topology)
Type of Resources	Content and links
Authorship of Site	Private individual (Alexander Bogomolny)
Navigation	Good
Visual Appeal	Very good
Interactive Activity	Some (following instructions to make variations on a Moebius strip and doing interactive activities)

Moebius Strip contains an in-depth discussion of the Moebius strip and variations of it. The provided graphics are excellent for visualizing what the various strips look like. Instructions for making the Moebius strip and some variations of it are provided. The site also contains information and activities for other mathematical topics (for example, probability).

TITLE: **Logical Art and the Art of Logic**

http://pubweb.northwestern.edu/~gbuehler/index0.htm	
Intended Audience	Teachers and students
Grade Level	Elementary grades and up
Curricular Fit	Geometry (pentominoes)
Type of Resources	Content
Authorship of Site	Private individual (Guenter Albrecht-Buehler)
Navigation	Good
Visual Appeal	Very good
Interactive Activity	Some (when downloading and using a DOS pentominoe program)

Logical Art and the Art of Logic should be entitled "An in-depth look into pentominoes and other similar creatures". It offers a comprehensive discussion of pentominoes (five squares joined together along a side in all possible ways) which includes graphics. There also is collection of artwork that involves pentominoes. The artwork is the section of the site that would be directly relevant to students. A DOS computer program can be downloaded. It generates 6 × 10 pentominoe solutions manually or automatically and does other entertaining things.

TITLE: **Math art gallery**

http://www-math.sci.kun.nl:80/math/knopen/art_gallery.html	
Intended Audience	Teachers and students
Grade Level	Elementary grades and up
Curricular Fit	Topology, chaos theory
Type of Resources	Content and links
Authorship of Site	Wiskunde, The Netherlands
Navigation	Good
Visual Appeal	Very good
Interactive Activity	Some (when downloading source files of the graphics)

Math art gallery provides a collection of marvelous images derived from topology and chaos theory. For example, there are images of knots (including animation) and complex spirals. These images can be used to help students understand that mathematics is much more than "number stuff" and to motivate them to learn about the mathematics that underlies the images.

TITLE: **The Mathematics of Cartography**

http://math.rice.edu/~lanius/pres/map/	
Intended Audience	Students and teachers
Grade Level	Upper elementary grades and up
Curricular Fit	Geometry, number concepts
Type of Resources	Content and links
Authorship of Site	Rice University (Cynthia Lanius)
Navigation	Very good
Visual Appeal	Good
Interactive Activity	Some (when determining distance, latitude, and longitude)

The Mathematics of Cartography contains comprehensive and extensive information on maps and the mathematics involved in them. It provides information on what maps are, the history of mapmaking, and the mathematics of maps (e.g., scale, projections). An interactive tool allows students to obtain information on the distance between two places, and the latitude and longitude of each. There is information on map-related careers and lessons on maps available for teachers. The site also contains links to other map-related sites. This is the place to start your search for information and lessons on maps.

Middle Years to High School Sites

TITLE: **World! Of Numbers**

http://ping4.ping.be/~ping6758/index.shtml	
Intended Audience	Teachers and students
Grade Level	Middle years and high school
Curricular Fit	Number concepts and theory
Type of Resources	Content and links
Authorship of Site	Private individual (Patrick De Geest, Belgium)
Navigation	Good
Visual Appeal	Good
Interactive Activity	Some (when solving puzzles)

World! Of Numbers contains extensive information on palindromic numbers (they read the same forward and backward). It also includes information on prime numbers and magic squares. This site is well worth visiting for teachers who desire in-depth information on palindromes and related ideas. The information can be used for designing interesting investigative activities.

TITLE: **How many? A Dictionary of Units of Measurement**

http://www.unc.edu/~rowlett/units/	
Intended Audience	Teachers and students
Grade Level	Middle years and high school
Curricular Fit	Measurement
Type of Resources	Content
Authorship of Site	University of North Carolina at Chapel Hill (Russ Rowlett)
Navigation	Good
Visual Appeal	Satisfactory
Interactive Activity	None

How many? A Dictionary of Units of Measurement provides definitions of metric and non-metric units of measurement and additional information related to the units.

TITLE: **JC's Decimal-to-Mayan Converter**

http://trillian.mit.edu/~jc/conv/d2m?number=20&orient=V&layout=H	
Intended Audience	Teachers and students
Grade Level	Middle years and up
Curricular Fit	Number systems
Type of Resources	Content and some links
Authorship of Site	Unknown (private individual)
Navigation	Good
Visual Appeal	Satisfactory
Interactive Activity	Some (when entering numbers)

JC's Decimal-to-Mayan Converter offers a base 10 to Mayan number conversion tool. The student enters a base 10 number such as 123 and the converter provides the Mayan equivalent. The site also includes links to other Mayan sites.

TITLE: **The story of pi**

http://www.geocities.com/CapeCanaveral/Lab/3550/pi.htm	
Intended Audience	Teachers and students
Grade Level	Middle years and up
Curricular Fit	Number systems
Type of Resources	Content and some links
Authorship of Site	Lazarus Mudehwe
Navigation	Good
Visual Appeal	Satisfactory
Interactive Activity	Some (when entering numbers)

The story of pi contains information on the history of pi, approximations for it, and links to sites that concern it.

TITLE: **The Fractory: An Interactive Tool for Creating and Exploring Fractals**

http://tqd.advanced.org/3288/	
Intended Audience	Students and teachers
Grade Level	Middle years and up
Curricular Fit	Chaos theory, geometry (fractals)
Type of Resources	Content and links
Authorship of Site	ThinkQuest
Navigation	Very good
Visual Appeal	Very good
Interactive Activity	Some (when creating fractals via the site)

The Fractory: An Interactive Tool for Creating and Exploring Fractals is designed to teach about fractals—what they are and how to design them—but it also allows for discovery of some of their features. Fractals are one of the latest hot topics in mathematics (a part of chaos theory). They show an order in seemingly random things, and provide tools which can be used to predict weather and to draw graphics that look like the real thing. This site provides spectacular graphics of fractal objects and is the place to go to for extensive and useful information on fractals. The site also provides opportunities to create fractals at an interactive fractal creation center and to design and display fractals that have been invented by a student or teacher. These creations can be posted on a bulletin board.

TITLE: **The Largest Known Primes**

http://www.utm.edu/research/primes/largest.html	
Intended Audience	Students and teachers
Grade Level	Middle years and up
Curricular Fit	Number concepts
Type of Resources	Content and links
Authorship of Site	University of Tennessee (Chris K. Caldwell)
Navigation	Good
Visual Appeal	Good
Interactive Activity	None

The Largest Known Primes is a site that provides information on prime numbers (what they are, why they are important, types of primes, the largest known) and links to other sites on primes. This site is a good place to begin when seeking current information about prime numbers.

TITLE: **The MacTutor History of Mathematics archive**

http://www-groups.dcs.st-and.ac.uk/~history/	
Intended Audience	Teachers and students
Grade Level	Middle years and up
Curricular Fit	A variety of mathematics topics
Type of Resources	Content and links
Authorship of Site	School of Mathematical and Computational Sciences, University of St. Andrews
Navigation	Good
Visual Appeal	Satisfactory
Interactive Activity	Minimal (via e-mail)

The MacTutor History of Mathematics archive provides information on the history of mathematics (for example, Babylonian and Egyptian mathematics, the history of the four-color theorem), information on a large number of mathematicians, and recent articles on Islamic and Greek mathematics. Some of the information includes maps that assist in visualizing where the topic developed or the mathematician lived. It also provides information on famous mathematical curves (for example, cardioid, Fermat's spiral), and includes JAVA-generated graphics of the curves.

TITLE: **Print a Googolplex**

http://www.informatik.uni-frankfurt.de/~fp/Tools/Googool.html	
Intended Audience	Students and teachers
Grade Level	Upper middle years and up
Curricular Fit	Number theory
Type of Resources	Content and links
Authorship of Site	University of Frankfurt (Frank Pilhofer)
Navigation	Good
Visual Appeal	Satisfactory
Interactive Activity	None

Print a Googolplex provides information on two very large numbers—a googol and a googolplex—and links to information on other large numbers. The site also offers access to a computer program written in C that prints large numbers (such as a googol). A related site is **Fun with Numbers The Home Page.** The URL for this site is: **http://www.newdream.net/~sage/old/numbers/**

High School Sites

TITLE: **Geometry in Action**

http://www.ics.uci.edu/~eppstein/geom.html	
Intended Audience	Teachers and students
Grade Level	11–12 and up
Curricular Fit	Geometry and its applications
Type of Resources	Links
Authorship of Site	University of California at Irvine (David Eppstein)
Navigation	Good
Visual Appeal	Satisfactory
Interactive Activity	Minimal (when submitting contributions)

Geometry in Action is a collection of links to sites that provide information on how ideas from discrete and computational geometry are involved in real-world applications. Brief descriptions are provided for many of those sites. The applications and the geometric questions that arise from them are described. The links are organized mainly by application (for example, architecture, computer-aided design, character recognition). A related site about geometry also worth visiting is: **http://www.ics.uci.edu/~eppstein/junkyard/teach.html**

TITLE: **Mathematics in Biology**

http://www.bio.brandeis.edu/biomath/top.html	
Intended Audience	Students and teachers
Grade Level	High school and up
Curricular Fit	A variety of topics
Type of Resources	Content and links
Authorship of Site	Geoffrey Dixon
Navigation	Good
Visual Appeal	Good
Interactive Activity	Some

Mathematics in Biology provides information on how mathematics plays a role in biological systems, including disease propagation and population growth. One goal of this site is to counteract the common view that mathematics plays only a minor role in biology. That may have been true once, but today the situation has substantially changed, with sophisticated mathematics playing an important role in modeling biological systems.

TITLE: **Cybergeezer's Lottery Page**

http://www.cybergeezer.com/lottery.html	
Intended Audience	Teachers and students
Grade Level	Mostly high school
Curricular Fit	Probability, statistics, and combinatorics
Type of Resources	Content
Authorship of Site	Cybergeezer
Navigation	Very good
Visual Appeal	Very good
Interactive Activity	None

Cybergeezer's Lottery Page contains comprehensive and extensive information on the mathematics of lotteries. It offers good insight into how probability, statistics, and combinations are involved in explaining the chances of winning a lottery.

TITLE: **LIFEPAGE**

http://members.aol.com/life1ine/life/	
Intended Audience	Teachers and students
Grade Level	High school
Curricular Fit	Mathematical modeling, chaos theory
Type of Resources	Content and some links
Authorship of Site	Robert Wainwright
Navigation	Good
Visual Appeal	Satisfactory
Interactive Activity	None

LIFEPAGE offers information on John Conway's game of life, a newsletter about the game, links to life sites, and interesting mathematical games and puzzles.

TITLE: **Erich's Packing Center**

http://www.stetson.edu/~efriedma/packing.html	
Intended Audience	Teachers and students
Grade Level	Mostly grade 12 (some possibilities for grades 5–11)
Curricular Fit	Geometry (2-D and 3-D packing)
Type of Resources	Content
Authorship of Site	Mathematics Department, Stetson University, FL (Erich Friedman)
Navigation	Good
Visual Appeal	Very good
Interactive Activity	None

Erich's Packing Center provides information on and solutions to 2-D and 3-D packing problems. It is of special interest to teachers looking for enrichment ideas at the grade 11/12 level. Some of the problems can be modified for use at middle years grade levels.

TITLE: **In a World of Order . . . Chaos Reigns!**

http://tqd.advanced.org/3120/	
Intended Audience	Teachers and students
Grade Level	High school
Curricular Fit	Chaos theory, probability
Type of Resources	Content
Authorship of Site	ThinkQuest organization
Navigation	Very Good
Visual Appeal	Very good
Interactive Activity	Minimal (when providing feedback on the site)

In a World of Order . . . Chaos Reigns! contains useful and interesting information on chaos theory (a recent development in mathematics). A major focus of chaos theory is predicting what happens in complex systems. A popular metaphor for this concerns the butterfly effect (a butterfly flapping its wings in Chicago can alter the weather in Los Angeles). The site explains, in fairly simple terms, the basic principles behind chaos theory and provides examples of its use in everyday life (e.g., in designing a better washing machine). It also includes animated samples of fractals, which provide a visual sense of one portion of chaos theory. The site is worth visiting for a good peek into chaos theory.

TITLE: **An Outline of the History of Game Theory**

http://william-king.www.drexel.edu/top/class/histf.html	
Intended Audience	Teachers and students
Grade Level	High school
Curricular Fit	Mathematical game theory
Type of Resources	Content and links
Authorship of Site	Paul Walker
Navigation	Good
Visual Appeal	Satisfactory
Interactive Activity	None

An Outline of the History of Game Theory provides extensive information on the history of game theory, a branch of mathematics that has applications in such fields as economics.

TITLE: **Euclid's Elements**

http://aleph0.clarku.edu/~djoyce/java/elements/elements.html	
Intended Audience	Teachers and students
Grade Level	High school
Curricular Fit	Geometry
Type of Resources	Content and links
Authorship of Site	Clark University (D. E. Joyce)
Navigation	Very Good
Visual Appeal	Very good
Interactive Activity	None

Euclid's Elements contains *Euclid's Elements*, one of the most influential works of mathematics in the history of humankind. The beauty of *Euclid's Elements* lies in its logical development of geometry and other branches of mathematics. JAVA Applets are used to provide images of the geometry, which helps bring the elements alive. The text of all 13 books is complete, and all of the figures are illustrated using the Geometry Applet, even the three-dimensional ones in the last three books on solid geometry. This is a good site to visit for a deep look into a work that is an important part of the history of the development of mathematics.

Starting | Developing | Exchanging | Participating | Projects | Resources | Home | Texthome

Graph Your Favorite...

Favorite Food

An Internet collaboration by:
Wendy Snyder, Syracuse, NY, USA, and
Nancy Schubert, Hilltop Primary School, Mound, MN, USA

Students in eight participating classes voted weekly on a new **Favorite:**

Pets...Holidays...Sports...School Subjects...Food.

The data was tallied separately for boys and for girls. Eight Grade 2, 4, and 6 classrooms in Michigan, Minnesota, Canada, Australia, and California answered sent their data to the project coordinator. The coordinator compiled the results on a ClarisWorks 4.0 spreadsheet and e-mailed it to everyone for further analysis. For participants without ClarisWorks 4.0, a desktop photograph of the spreadsheet was provided.

Students used the data in raw form to make their own spreadsheets, both manually and by computer. They also made computer bar graphs and pie graphs as well as manually drawn bar graphs. Then they analyzed the graphs and drew conclusions. Before seeing the data, students made their own outcome predictions and compared them to the actual data.

★ **The Project Plan**
★ **Compiling and Presenting the Data**: Sample spreadsheets and graphs.

Courtesy of NickNacks Telecollaborate!

Graph Your Favorite . . .
http://www1.minn.net:80/~schubert/Graph.html

STATISTICS

The following sites involve statistics. The sites provide a comprehensive sampling of the resources available on the Internet for this category. Some sites contain extensive data (for example, weather data, U.S. Census data). Others provide links to schools around the globe, which can be used as a pipeline for gathering first-hand data from people and places far from the classroom. There also are a few gateway sites that provide links to a large variety of data sites. Some sites provide helpful information on setting up collaborative data management projects (and access to such projects) and on teaching statistics.

Elementary to High School Sites

TITLE: **U. S. Census Bureau Home Page**

http://www.census.gov/	
Intended Audience	Teachers and students
Grade Level	K–12
Curricular Fit	Data management (statistics)
Type of Resources	Content
Authorship of Site	Government of the United States
Navigation	Very good
Visual Appeal	Very good
Interactive Activity	Minimal (via e-mail)

U. S. Census Bureau Home Page is the place for social, demographic, and economic data on the United States. It allows students access to relevant data that can be analyzed and interpreted. The site also offers teaching activities.

TITLE: **Statistics Canada**

http://www.statcan.ca/start.html	
Intended Audience	Teachers
Grade Level	K–12
Curricular Fit	Data management (statistics)
Type of Resources	Content
Authorship of Site	Government of Canada
Navigation	Good
Visual Appeal	Good
Interactive Activity	Some (when doing interactive activities)

Statistics Canada is the place for data on Canada. It also offers teachers education resources (programs and products) to integrate Canadian statistical information into teaching and learning. For example, the site contains lesson plans and teacher's kits.

TITLE: **Other Statistical Web Sites**

http://www.statcan.ca/english/reference/servrs.htm	
Intended Audience	Teachers and students
Grade Level	K–12
Curricular Fit	Data management (statistics)
Type of Resources	Links
Authorship of Site	Government of Canada
Navigation	Good
Visual Appeal	Satisfactory
Interactive Activity	None

Other statistical Web sites is a large collection of links to data sites of all the Canadian provinces and territories and to data sites of other countries. For example, there are links to Statistics Finland, Statistics New Zealand, and Australian Bureau of Statistics.

TITLE: **Web66: International School Web Site Registry**

http://web66.coled.umn.edu/schools.html	
Intended Audience	Teachers
Grade Level	K–12
Curricular Fit	Data management (statistics) and other mathematics topics
Type of Resources	Links
Authorship of Site	University of Minnesota
Navigation	Good
Visual Appeal	Good
Interactive Activity	Some (when contacting the schools)

Web66: International School Web Site Registry provides extensive links to school sites around the world. For example, there are links to schools in the United States, Canada, Japan, France, Turkey, Honduras, and the Marshall Islands. Communicating with such school sites can provide opportunities to obtain data for data management purposes, and to collaborate on data management projects and on learning mathematics. Clickable maps are provided for the major regions of the world (e.g., Europe). These maps are an added benefit in that they can help students gain a sense of where the school's country is located.

TITLE: **Web66 International School Web Registry**

http://web66.coled.umn.edu/Schools/Lists/Math.html	
Intended Audience	Teachers and students
Grade Level	K–12
Curricular Fit	Data management (statistics) and other mathematics topics
Type of Resources	Links to schools
Authorship of Site	University of Minnesota
Navigation	Good
Visual Appeal	Satisfactory
Interactive Activity	Minimal (via e-mail)

Web66 International School Web Registry is a collection of links to elementary and secondary math magnet schools (as well as some links to mathematics organizations). The links offer possible collaboration between classrooms on data management projects and on mathematical learning in general.

TITLE: **Interesting Weather Internet Sites**

http://www.ncsa.uiuc.edu/edu/RSE/RSEred/InternetSites.html	
Intended Audience	Teachers and students
Grade Level	4 and up
Curricular Fit	Data management (statistics)
Type of Resources	Links
Authorship of Site	University of Illinois at Urbana-Champaign
Navigation	Very good
Visual Appeal	Good
Interactive Activity	None

Interesting Weather Internet Sites is a gateway to a variety of websites that provide weather information that includes numerical data and weather maps. Teachers can identify appropriate data sites from the links and then have students access them to obtain data for weather-related data management projects.

TITLE: **Automated Weather Source**

http://aws.com/comps/corp/default.asp?showlogo=1&boturl=http://aws.com/instaweather.asp	
Intended Audience	Teachers and students
Grade Level	4 and up
Curricular Fit	Data management (statistics)
Type of Resources	Links and content
Authorship of Site	Commercial (Automated Weather Service)
Navigation	Satisfactory
Visual Appeal	Very good
Interactive Activity	Some (when gathering real-time weather data)

Automated Weather Source has valuable possibilities for integrating science and mathematics. It provides an opportunity for a school to become part of a network of weather stations. Software from Automated Weather Service (AWS) is required for this. It allows all AWS automated weather stations to be connected to the Internet. The on-line AWS weather service generates "true up-to-the-second real-time" weather data from locations throughout the world (for example, United States, Canada, Australia, New Zealand). Sites that are part of the AWS network can access this data.

Elementary Grades Sites

TITLE: **Graph Your Favorite . . .**

http://www1.minn.net:80/~schubert/Graph.html	
Intended Audience	Teachers and students
Grade Level	2–6
Curricular Fit	Data management (statistics)
Type of Resources	Content and links to other classrooms
Authorship of Site	NickNacks Collaborate! (MN)
Navigation	Good
Visual Appeal	Good
Interactive Activity	Some (when collaborating on data management projects)

Graph Your Favorite . . . promotes collaboration on data management projects. The project described at the site involved students from eight elementary
classrooms collaborating in gathering and analyzing data on a variety of subjects
such as "Favorite: Pet, Holiday, Sport, School Subject, Food." The data was sent to
the project coordinator who compiled the results on a Clarisworks 4.0 spreadsheet
and e-mailed the spreadsheet, or a PICT file of the spreadsheet, to all participants
for further analysis. Teachers can use the project information to generate similar
projects. The links to other elementary schools that are provided at this site can be
used to initiate collaborative projects.

TITLE: **National Center for Education Statistics**

http://nces.ed.gov/nceskids/	
Intended Audience	Students primarily
Grade Level	4–7
Curricular Fit	Statistics and probability
Type of Resources	Content
Authorship of Site	National Center for Education Statistics (NCES)
Navigation	Good
Visual Appeal	Good
Interactive Activity	Extensive

National Center for Education Statistics offers information and interactive
games and activities related to using and appreciating statistics. For example,
the site includes a dice rolling activity that graphs the simulated results of rolling
the dice.

TITLE: **Welcome to the Grade 6 Home Page**

http://www.mbnet.mb.ca/~jfinch/	
Intended Audience	Students
Grade Level	5/6
Curricular Fit	Data management (statistics)
Type of Resources	Content and links
Authorship of Site	A grade 6 class in Dauphin, Manitoba
Navigation	Good
Visual Appeal	Good
Interactive Activity	Some (via e-mail)

Welcome to the Grade 6 Home Page offers an opportunity to communicate (via e-mail) with a grade 6 class for a variety of purposes. In relation to learning mathematics, one purpose would be gathering data for and/or collaborating on a data management project. The site includes math problems created by students from grades 3 to 6.

Middle Years to High School Sites

TITLE: **Canadiana—The Canadian Resource Page**

http://www.cs.cmu.edu/Unofficial/Canadiana/	
Intended Audience	Teachers and students
Grade Level	Middle years and up
Curricular Fit	Data management (statistics)
Type of Resources	Links
Authorship of Site	Private individual (Stewart Clamen)
Navigation	Good
Visual Appeal	Satisfactory
Interactive Activity	None

Canadiana—The Canadian Resource Page provides a large collection of links to sites that contain data (numerical and non-numerical) on Canada. For example, there are links to Canadian currency exchange rates with other currencies, postal codes, Canadian-based on-line publications (newspapers, journals and the like), Canadian economic indicators, Supreme Court of Canada decisions, and so on. This site could be described as the gateway to everything you want to know about Canada.

TITLE: **K–12 Statistics**

http://www.mste.uiuc.edu/stat/stat.html	
Intended Audience	Teachers
Grade Level	Middle Years and up
Curricular Fit	Statistics and probability
Type of Resources	Links
Authorship of Site	University of Illinois at Urbana-Champaign, MSTE
Navigation	Good
Visual Appeal	Good
Interactive Activity	Some (when doing some of the activities)

K–12 Statistics is a collection of links to sites of interesting activities and data sets for statistics. The activities are suited mostly for middle and senior years students. Some of the activities involve interaction (e.g., a computer program can be downloaded that will generate data). The site is useful to teachers looking for classroom examples of how to apply the NCTM statistics standard and to teachers who are looking for novel and intriguing statistics activities.

High School Sites

TITLE: **Native American Documents Project**

http://www.csusm.edu/projects/nadp/nadp.htm	
Intended Audience	Teachers and students
Grade Level	High school
Curricular Fit	Data management (statistics)
Type of Resources	Content
Authorship of Site	California State University at San Marcos
Navigation	Good
Visual Appeal	Satisfactory
Interactive Activity	None

Native American Documents Project provides three types of information about Native Americans: published reports, allotment data, and indexed and undexed documents. The allotment data is the most useful for data management purposes as it includes quantitative data about the results of allotment. (Allotment was the process that allowed most of the land base left to Native Americans by the late 19th century to pass into other hands.)

TITLE: **The Data and Story Library**

http://lib.stat.cmu.edu/DASL/	
Intended Audience	Teachers and students
Grade Level	High school
Curricular Fit	Statistics
Type of Resources	Content
Authorship of Site	DASL Project, Cornell University
Navigation	Good
Visual Appeal	Good
Interactive Activity	Some (when accessing the data files and when submitting stories)

The Data and Story Library is designed to help teachers locate and identify data files for teaching statistics. It contains two types of resources to illustrate statistical concepts: stories and data files. Each data file has one or more associated stories. The data can be downloaded and accessed by most statistical programs. Each story applies a particular statistical method to a set of data. The stories come from a variety of areas including archaeology, biology, environmental science, nutrition, and psychology. For example there is an archaeology story about four measurements that were made of male Egyptian skulls from a time period ranging from 4000 B.C. to 150 A.D. The question of interest was if there are any differences in the skull sizes between the time periods and if they show any changes with time. This question is important to addressing the theory that a change in skull size over time is evidence of Egyptians interbreeding with immigrant populations over the years.

TITLE: **UCLA Department of Statistics**

http://www.stat.ucla.edu/	
Intended Audience	Teachers
Grade Level	High school and beyond
Curricular Fit	Statistics
Type of Resources	Content and links
Authorship of Site	Statistics Department, UCLA (Jan de Leeuw)
Navigation	Good
Visual Appeal	Satisfactory
Interactive Activity	Some (through a free electronic consulting service)

UCLA Department of Statistics provides access to information on statistics, to databases that could be used for teaching statistics (e.g., demographic data), to publications that can be useful for teaching statistics, and to links that involve statistics. The site is especially worth visiting for those who are seeking information related to higher level statistics.

Topics in Mathematics	Software
Teaching materials, software, WWW links organized by Mathematical Topics. Searchable database.	Public domain and shareware software for Macintosh, Windows (98, 95, 3.1 and (MS)DOS) computers and for multi-platforms (incl. UNIX) is addition to links to other software sites.
Teaching Materials	**Other Math Archives Features**
• Calculus Resources On-line • Contests and Competitions • Graphing Calculators • K-12 Teaching Materials • Visual Calculus • etc.	• Electronic Proceedings of the ICTCM Conferences • UTK Mathematical Life Sciences Archives • Project NExT • PC Mathematics • Archives of Mailing Lists • SIMMS RA • TIMATYC • etc.
Other Links	**Search the Math Archives**
Links to other mathematics related sites and sites of interest to students and teachers of mathematics.	Full text searching of all pages and documents on the Math Archives.
What's New on the Math Archives	**Math Archives Information**
A listing of the current month's and previous month's additions to the Math Archives.	Goals, financial support, personnel, information on submitting materials to the Math Archives, etc.

Hosted on SunSITE, University of Tennessee, Knoxville.

Courtesy of Mathematics Archives, University of Tennessee

Math Archives
http://archives.math.utk.edu:80/

COMPREHENSIVE GATEWAYS

A gateway site consists primarily of links to other sites. The gateway sites included here point to a wide range of resources involving mathematics across the various grade levels (and sometimes other subject areas). If you are uncertain of what you are looking for and are willing to spend some time browsing, then a gateway site is a good place to begin. It is the equivalent of a search engine that has greatly narrowed the zone of possibilities.

Elementary to High School Sites

TITLE: **Math Archives**

http://archives.math.utk.edu:80/	
Intended Audience	Teachers
Grade Level	K–12
Curricular Fit	A variety of mathematics topics
Type of Resources	Links
Authorship of Site	Mathematics Archives (University of Tennessee)
Navigation	Good
Visual Appeal	Good
Interactive Activity	Minimal (contributions to the database are welcome)

Math Archives is a major gateway site with six categories of links to sites available. "Topics in Mathematics" provides links to mathematics publications, including journals. "Software" provides links to public domain and shareware software sites (for example, Cabri demo programs). "Teaching Materials" provides links to resources on K–12 lessons and materials and more. "Other Math Archive Features" provides links to professional organizations and conference proceedings. "Other Links" provides links to other mathematics-related sites that are of interest to students and teachers. "What's New on the Math Archives" provides a listing of the current month's and previous months' additions to the database. The site features full text searching of all pages and documents in its database.

TITLE: **Lightspan Study WEB Mathematics**

http://www.studyweb.com/Mathematics/toc.htm	
Intended Audience	Teachers
Grade Level	K–12
Curricular Fit	A variety of mathematics topics
Type of Resources	Links
Authorship of Site	Lightspan Inc.
Navigation	Good
Visual Appeal	Good
Interactive Activity	None

Lightspan Study WEB Mathematics is a major gateway site. Its links are organized into nine categories (for example, arithmetic, geometry, advanced math). Each category lists many links. The site also features a "Mathematics Featured Site of the Month" and provides a brief description of it.

TITLE:　**Math Links on the World Wide Web**

http://www.roseville.k12.mn.us/rahs/media/math.html	
Intended Audience	Teachers and students
Grade Level	K–12
Curricular Fit	A variety of mathematical topics
Type of Resources	Links
Authorship of Site	Roseville Area High School
Navigation	Good
Visual Appeal	Satisfactory
Interactive Activity	None

Math Links on the World Wide Web is a gateway to a large variety of websites that include other subject areas, especially science. The site contains a category of links to sites for students and a category of links to sites for teachers. The site is a useful place to begin when looking for ideas for teaching mathematics.

TITLE:　**Florida SMART: Mathematics**

http://www.floridasmart.com/subjects/math.htm	
Intended Audience	Teachers, students, and parents
Grade Level	K–12
Curricular Fit	A variety of mathematical topics
Type of Resources	Links
Authorship of site	FloridaSMART
Navigation	Good
Visual Appeal	Good
Interactive Activity	None

Florida SMART: Mathematics is a gateway to many subject areas including mathematics. The mathematics section includes links to lessons, activities, and information about such topics as algebra, fractals, basic mathematics, geometry, and history/mathematicians.

TITLE: **LessonPlans4Teachers**

http://www.theeducatorsnetwork.com/lessons/index.htm	
Intended Audience	Teachers
Grade Level	K–12
Curricular Fit	A variety of mathematical topics
Type of Resources	Links
Authorship of Site	Educators Network, Inc.
Navigation	Very good
Visual Appeal	Satisfactory
Interactive Activity	Some (when contributing to the "school of the month" and the "featured site" features and when providing feedback)

LessonPlans4Teachers contains a searchable database of links to teaching resources for a variety of subject areas, including mathematics. It offers five tools to use for searching for a resource: a generic search engine, a lesson plan search engine, a grade/subject search, a top ten list by subject search, and a best of the rest search. The site's search tools have been configured to maximize success in finding suitable resources. The goal is to create the best lesson plan directory and search site and user input is welcome to help attain that goal.

TITLE: **Sites for Teachers: Math**

http://learningpage.superb.net/sft/resources_sharp/math/math.html	
Intended Audience	Teachers and students
Grade Level	K–12
Curricular Fit	A variety of mathematical topics
Type of Resources	Links
Authorship of Site	Morgan-Cain & Associates and Vicki and Richard Sharp
Navigation	Very good
Visual Appeal	Satisfactory
Interactive Activity	Minimal (contributions of links are welcomed)

Sites for Teachers: Math is a well-organized and comprehensive collection of links to other sites that have a variety of resources. There are six categories of links: "Lesson Plans," "Ideas and Activities," "Applications," "Board Games," "Puzzles and Problems," and "Organizations."

TITLE: **Mathematics and Computer Science Hotlist**

http://sln.fi.edu/tfi/hotlists/math.html	
Intended Audience	Teachers
Grade Level	K–12
Curricular Fit	A variety of mathematics topics
Type of Resources	Links
Authorship of Site	The Franklin Institute
Navigation	Good
Visual Appeal	Satisfactory
Interactive Activity	None

Mathematics and Computer Science Hotlist is an organized list of links to sites on the Internet that mathematics educators should find useful. The sites have been screened for their educational appropriateness, helping take some of the guesswork out of searches. To make the list, the resources at a site need to stimulate creative thinking and learning about mathematics. Two examples of the resources to which links have been provided are: A+ Math, and Circles of Light: The Mathematics of Rainbows.

TITLE: **Canada's SchoolNet: Learning Resources: Mathematics**

http://www.schoolnet.ca/home/e/resources/browse_results.asp? SECTION=0&SUBJECT=28&LangID=1&SEARCH=index.asp	
Intended Audience	Teachers
Grade Level	K–12
Curricular Fit	A variety of mathematics topics
Type of Resources	Links and content
Authorship of Site	SchoolNet (Canada)
Navigation	Good
Visual Appeal	Good
Interactive Activity	None

Canada's SchoolNet: Learning Resources: Mathematics contains links to a variety of good sites (for example, Appetizers and Lessons for Mathematics and Reason, Bluedog Can Count!, Gallery of Interactive Geometry). The links include descriptions of the sites.

TITLE: **Welcome to Mathematics Education Resource Page**

http://www.uwo.ca/edu/math/	
Intended Audience	Teachers
Grade Level	K–12 and beyond
Curricular Fit	A variety of mathematics topics
Type of Resources	Links and content
Authorship of Site	Faculty of Education, University of Western Ontario
Navigation	Satisfactory
Visual Appeal	Good
Interactive Activity	Some

Welcome to Mathematics Education Resource Page is mostly a collection of links to a variety of sites (for example, lessons/activities, professional organizations). It contains other useful resources (designed mostly for the high school level) in the form of a collection of computer software programs that can be downloaded free of charge. Some examples of these programs are a program that develops the relationship between a unit circle and the trigonometric functions and a program that simulates the Buffon needle experiment to determine a value for pi.

OTHER MATH-RELATED MATTERS

TITLE: **Math in Daily Life**

http://www.learner.org/exhibits/dailymath/	
Intended Audience	Teachers and students
Grade Level	5–12
Curricular Fit	A variety of mathematics topics
Type of Resources	Content and links
Authorship of Site	Annenberg/CPB
Navigation	Good
Visual Appeal	Good
Interactive Activity	None

Math in daily Life presents information and links about how mathematics affects daily decision making, including information on population growth, home decorating, and savings and credit.

TITLE: **Calculators On-line Center**

http://www-sci.lib.uci.edu/HSG/RefCalculators.html	
Intended Audience	Teachers and students
Grade Level	Upper elementary to post-secondary
Curricular Fit	Calculators, statistics, number theory
Type of Resources	Links
Authorship of Site	Jim Martindale
Navigation	Good
Visual Appeal	Satisfactory
Interactive Activity	None

Calculators On-line Center is a gateway to a variety of on-line calculators for a variety of applications, including business, science, and mathematics. For example, it provides a link to a calculator that converts base 10 numerals into Chinese numerals and a link to a calculator that performs sampling analysis.

TITLE: **The National Math Trail**

http://www.nationalmathtrail.org/	
Intended Audience	Teachers and students
Grade Level	K–12
Curricular Fit	A variety of mathematical topics
Type of Resources	Content
Authorship of Site	National Math Trail
Navigation	Very good
Visual Appeal	Very good
Interactive Activity	Some (when submitting resources)

The National Math Trail provides K–12 teachers and students an opportunity to discover and share the math that exists in their communities. Students create one or more math problems that relate to what they find in their communities. Teachers submit the problems to the National Math Trail site, along with whatever can be adapted to the Internet (e.g. photos, drawings, sound recordings, videos).

Submissions are posted to the site and are indexed according to grade level and math topic and remain on the site for access by educators, students and parents.

TITLE: **Welcome to Bamdad's Math Comics Page**

http://www.csun.edu/~hcmth014/comics.html	
Intended Audience	Teachers and students
Grade Level	K–12
Curricular Fit	A variety of mathematical topics
Type of Resources	Content
Authorship of Site	California State University (Bamdad Samii)
Navigation	Good
Visual Appeal	Very good
Interactive Activity	None (except through contributing new comics)

Welcome to Bamdad's Math Comics Page is a collection of over 150 mathematics-related cartoons that can be used to stimulate discussion about attitudes towards mathematics and about mathematical concepts. While not a lesson plan/activity site per se, teachers can use the cartoons found at this site to generate ideas for interesting lessons and activities.

TITLE: **Weather Here and There**

http://www.ncsa.uiuc.edu/edu/RSE/RSEred/WeatherHome.html	
Intended Audience	Teachers
Grade Level	4–6
Curricular Fit	Data management, patterning
Type of Resources	Content
Authorship of Site	University of Illinois at Urbana-Champaign
Navigation	Good
Visual Appeal	Good
Interactive Activity	Some (via e-mail collaboration)

Weather Here and There contains an integrated weather unit that incorporates the Internet and hands-on collaborative, problem-solving activities. Six lessons integrate mathematics, science, geography, and language arts in learning about weather phenomena. Students can become involved in collaborative problem solving by communicating via e-mail as well as by joining projects offered on the Internet.

TITLE: **20 Kids * 20 Kites * 20 Minutes**

http://www.aloha.net/~bigwind/20kidskites.html	
Intended Audience	Teachers and students
Grade Level	4–6
Curricular Fit	Geometry and measurement
Type of Resources	Content
Authorship of site	Big Wind Kite Factory (HI)
Navigation	Very good
Visual Appeal	Good
Interactive Activity	Some (through e-mail when commenting or asking for more information about kites)

20 Kids * 20 Kites * 20 Minutes provides information on making a kite. Teachers can use the information to stimulate learning about geometry and to have students make practical use of their geometry and measurement skills.

TITLE: **SuperKids Educational Software Review**

http://www.superkids.com/aweb/pages/reviews/math1/sw_sum1.shtml	
Intended Audience	Teachers and parents
Grade Level	K–6
Curricular Fit	A variety of mathematics topics
Type of Resources	Content
Authorship of Site	Commercial (Knowledge Share LLC)
Navigation	Good
Visual Appeal	Good
Interactive Activity	None

SuperKids Educational Software Review provides comprehensive information on some mathematics software (for example: Carmen Sandiego Math Detective). The information includes a description of the software, its ease of use, and recommended grade level(s). The reviews offer positive as well as negative comments about the software.

TITLE: **Math and Children's Literature**

http://www.carolhurst.com/subjects/math/math.html	
Intended Audience	Teachers
Grade Level	K–6
Curricular Fit	A variety of mathematical topics and integration with children's literature
Type of Resources	Links and content
Authorship of Site	Commercial (Carol Hurst)
Navigation	Good
Visual Appeal	Good
Interactive Activity	Minimal (via e-mail)

Math and Children's Literature provides information on children's literature that involves mathematical concepts. It is useful for anyone interested in using children's literature to support the teaching of mathematics.

TITLE: **MAA Online: Career Profiles**

http://www.maa.org/careers/index.html	
Intended Audience	Teachers and students
Grade Level	Middle years and high school
Curricular Fit	A variety of topics
Type of Resources	Content
Authorship of Site	American Mathematical Association
Navigation	Good
Visual Appeal	Satisfactory
Interactive Activity	None

MAA Online: Career Profiles provides essays, written by people who use mathematics on the job, that describe why a background in mathematics is useful.

CHAPTER SUMMARY

This chapter contains an annotated listing of more than 100 websites that provide resources for teaching mathematics in the form of lessons and activities, problems, mathematics content, statistics, comprehensive gateways, and other math-related matters. The resources will help you to teach in ways that are consistent with the standards developed by the National Council of Teachers of Mathematics (NCTM).

CHAPTER 4

Links to Professional Development Resources

Courtesy of the National Council of Teachers of Mathematics

NCTM.org
http://www.nctm.org

- Associations, Organizations, Projects, Centers
- Information on Reform
- Information on Assessment

- Collaboration
- Gender Concerns
- Multicultural and Minority Groups Concerns

The Internet makes it possible for teachers to address many of their professional development needs without having to leave home or the office (so to speak). This chapter is devoted to websites that offer professional development services that can facilitate deeper thinking about mathematics education.

By accessing these sites, teachers can initiate and engage in a variety of professional development endeavors. For example, teachers can talk to other teachers about issues and concerns via e-mail and bulletin board groups. They can read about current efforts at reforming mathematics education and some of the issues pertaining to those efforts. Teachers can collaborate with each other on projects that reflect the NCTM's *Standards and Principles for School Mathematics* and, thereby, have an opportunity to engage in deeper discussion about implementing them.

This chapter introduces teachers to the opportunities for professional development that are available on the Internet. There are more than 50 professional development sites included, which are organized into six categories: Associations, Organizations, Projects, Centers; Information on Reform; Information on Assessment; Collaboration; Gender Concerns; and Multicultural and Minority Groups Concerns. Many of the included sites would fit into more than one category, but each site is listed only in the one that best fits it. The title and URL are provided for each listed site along with information on the site's pertinent features.

ASSOCIATIONS, ORGANIZATIONS, PROJECTS, CENTERS

Professional associations, organizations, projects, and centers offer a variety of professional development services for K–12 mathematics teachers. The following sites illustrate the kinds of services that are available.

Math Central

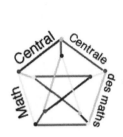

An Internet service for mathematics teachers and students from kindergarten to grade twelve.

Français

The Resource Room	Quandaries and Queries
The Resource Room is a place where mathematics educators can share resources, teaching ideas, lesson plans, etc. Visit The Resource Room to browse, use our Mathematics Glossaries, sample our resources or suggest a new resource. To search our database of resources enter a keyword below (for example fractions, tessellations,...) and click on search.	Do you have a mathematical question? Use a keyword to search our database of previous questions to see if you can find an answer, or send us your question and we will try to answer it.

Courtesy of the University of Regina, Regina, Saskatchewan

Math Central
http://MathCentral.uregina.ca/index.html

This site is sponsored by faculty members in the department of mathematics and statistics and the faculty of education at the University of Regina. It offers a meeting place for teachers to share resources and to allow them to carry on a dialogue among themselves (through "Teacher Talk"). Teachers are also encouraged to send teaching resources and suggestions for improving the site.

NCTM.org
http://www.nctm.org

This is the home page of the National Council of Teachers of Mathematics (NCTM). The site is the gateway to information on NCTM materials, meetings, membership, on-line classifieds, publications, and current events and projects. It is the place to go to look for in-depth information on reform and on the latest trends and issues in mathematics education.

Arkansas Council of Teachers of Mathematics
http://www.actm.net/

This is the website of the Arkansas Council of Teachers of Mathematics, a statewide organization of mathematics teachers from kindergarten through college level. The site provides news and information pertinent to teaching mathematics in Arkansas well as links to mathematics websites. A number of state and provincial teacher associations have web pages devoted to mathematics education and to information of local interest. The reader might want to search for the mathematics web page of his or her teacher association.

MAMT Manitoba Association of Mathematics Teachers
http://www.mamt.mb.ca/

This is the home page of the Manitoba Association of Mathematics Teachers. It offers information on workshops, mathematics contests, and its constitution. It provides links to related sites, access to publications, and an opportunity to participate in a public forum on mathematics teaching.

S.C.O.R.E. Math
http://score.k12.ca.us/

This site is sponsored by the California Technology Assistance Program and California County Superintendents Educational Services Association. It offers links to assessment and resource sites, in-service information, lesson plans and teaching activities (contributed by teachers), a discussion board, and e-mail access to the teachers of the SCORE mathematics resource development team.

AAMT 2001
http://www.AAMT.edu.au/

This site is sponsored by the Australian Association of Mathematics Teachers. It offers information, teaching resources and information on research projects.

Annenberg/CPB Learner.org
http://www.learner.org/

This site is sponsored by Annenberg/CPB Projects, an organization dedicated to helping schools and communities improve their mathematics and science programs. It offers print and electronic media and on-line resources that show concrete examples of good teaching and active learning in many different settings. It also offers "Journey North," a K–12 Internet-based project for use with students in the classroom or at home. The project engages students in a global study of wildlife migration and seasonal change. While this is a science project, it can easily be integrated with mathematics.

CMESG/GCEDM
http://plato.acadiau.ca/courses/educ/reid/cmesg/cmesg.html

This site is sponsored by the Canadian Mathematics Education Study Group (CMESG), an organization of mathematicians and mathematics educators. The site provides information on mathematics education in Canada and the CMESG journal, *For the Learning of Mathematics*, and links to mathematics resources.

Math Solutions® Online
http://www.mathsolutions.com/

This is a commercial site of Marilyn Burns Education Associates that offers mathematics teachers services such as courses and workshops, publications, on-line newsletters, and in-service programs. For example, the site offers assistance with developing teacher leadership expertise in mathematics.

Welcome to ENC
http://www.enc.org/

This is a website of the Eisenhower National Clearinghouse (ENC) for mathematics and science education. ENC is a part of the U.S. Department of Education's continuing efforts to reform K–12 mathematics and science education. The site provides information on teaching resources and links to them. It is also a gateway to information on reform.

AIMS Education Foundation
http://www.aimsedu.org/

This site is sponsored by the foundation, Activities Integrating Math & Science (AIMS). The site provides extensive links to mathematics resources, information on workshops and the AIMS magazine and product catalog, and an opportunity to exchange ideas about teaching mathematics and science.

CSI for Science and Math
http://www.luc.edu/schools/education/csi.htm

This site is sponsored by the Chicago System Initiative (CSI), a project funded by the National Science Foundation (NSF). The project's vision is that all children can and all children must learn science and mathematics, and learn to use technologies. This site provides information on CSI and reform, teaching resources (lessons and activities, software, articles), and links to resources for parents, teachers, and students.

The Geometry Center
http://www.geom.umn.edu:80/

This site is the home page of the University of Minnesota's mathematics research and education center. The site provides access to many resources for teaching geometry including information on current projects, a geometry reference archive, downloadable software, and teaching materials.

Centre for Teaching Mathematics
http://www.tech.plym.ac.uk/maths/CTMHOME/CTM.HTML

This is the website of an educational research, curriculum and resource development group of the University of Plymouth. The goal is to improve the teaching of all levels of mathematics through research and the development of appropriate teaching materials. The site provides information on activities, projects, publications, and enrichment programs (for the gifted).

Community Learning Network
http://www.cln.org/cln.html

This site is sponsored by the Open Learning Agency, an organization dedicated to helping K–12 teachers integrate technology into their classrooms. The site offers hundreds of menu pages with thousands of annotated links to educational websites, as well as over 100 on-site CLN resources. The menus provide access to resources that pertain to, for example, helping teachers understand how information technologies can assist students' learning. A good number of the links concern Internet-based or assisted resources for teaching mathematics.

Interactive Mathematics Program
http://www.mathimp.org/

This site is sponsored by Key Curriculum Press. The Interactive Mathematics Program (IMP) is a collaboration of mathematicians, teacher-educators, and teachers who have been working together since 1989 on both curriculum development and professional development for teachers (with the support of the National Science Foundation). The site offers a full four-year secondary mathematics curriculum and a rich professional development program for secondary mathematics teachers. This curriculum prepares students to use problem-solving skills in further education and on the job.

K–12 Mathematics Curriculum Center
http://www.edc.org/mcc/

This site is funded by the National Science Foundation (NSF) and offers seminars, resource guides, case study information, and consulting services to help facilitate discussion and decision making about implementing standards-based mathematics curricula.

CAMEL
http://camel.math.ca/

This site, sponsored by the Canadian Mathematical Society, offers a variety of resources including lessons, publications, and links to mathematics associations.

Pacific Institute for Mathematical Sciences
http://www.pims.math.ca/

This site is dedicated to the communication and dissemination of mathematical ideas through public outreach, mathematical education and training at all school levels, with a focus on the nations of the Pacific Rim. Its resources and information are intended for secondary and post-secondary educators.

The Mathematics Projects
http://www.ed.hawaii.edu/

This site provides access to curriculum projects that are based on research, that promote interaction among students, that support students' construction of knowledge, and that incorporate professional development and support services. One example is the "Reshaping Mathematics Project," a three-year curriculum intended for use by middle years students and teachers.

Anderson County Public Schools
http://www.acorns.k12.tn.us/

This site provides a variety of services to teachers and administrators. Some of it directly concerns mathematics. For example, the site provides mathematics lesson plans, opportunities to e-mail other teachers about teaching mathematics, and mathematics curriculum guides. Many school districts and divisions sponsor and maintain this kind of site. The reader might want to search for the website of his or her own local school district or division.

INFORMATION ON REFORM

The Internet has sites that provide information on reform in mathematics education. The information may be narrow or broad in scope. The following sites provide a sampling of the kinds of reading resources on reform that are available.

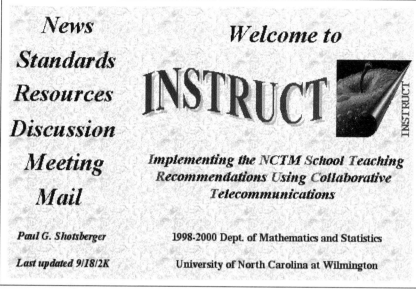

News

Standards

Resources

Discussion

Meeting

Mail

Welcome to

INSTRUCT

Implementing the NCTM School Teaching Recommendations Using Collaborative Telecommunications

Paul G. Shotsberger

Last updated 9/18/2K

1998-2000 Dept. of Mathematics and Statistics

University of North Carolina at Wilmington

Courtesy of the University of North Carolina at Wilmington (Paul G. Shotsberger)

Welcome to INSTRUCT
http://instruct.cms.uncwil.edu/

This site offers access to information on local events, a discussion group, and a live chat session, and provides links to mathematics resource sites and on-line help that is designed to assist teachers in understanding and implementing the NCTM's *Principles and Standards for School Mathematics.*

Mathematicians and Education Reform Forum
http://www.math.uic.edu/MER/

This site seeks the effective participation of mathematicians in mathematics education reform at the K–12, undergraduate, and graduate levels, and the recognition of the importance of these efforts to the teaching and learning of mathematics. It offers news, activities, and publications.

The Guide to Math & Science Reform
http://www.learner.org/theguide/

This Annenberg/CPB site offers a searchable database with information on projects, resources, and organizations devoted to reforming mathematics and science education.

McREL Eisenhower High Plains Consortium for Mathematics and Science
http://www.mcrel.org/hpc/

This site offers information and programs for promoting reform in mathematics education and links to teaching resources that reflect reform.

Mathematics Learning Forums
http://www.edc.org/CCT/mlf/MLF.html

This site invites participation in a growing nationwide group of educators interested in mathematics reform and the NCTM Standards. It provides an opportunity for elementary and middle school teachers to reflect on and refine their mathematics teaching practices through on-line seminars.

The K–12 Mathematics Curriculum Center
http://www.edc.org/mcc/

This site provides information on various aspects of reform, including NCTM *Standards*-based instruction and the role of technology. It offers curricula, materials and resources, seminars, and consulting services.

Welcome to Tales from the Electronic Frontier
http://www.wested.org/tales/

This is a WestEd site (a nonprofit research, development, and service agency). It offers access to a collection of 10 stories written by teachers. The stories or tales concern their classroom experiences using the Internet to teach science and mathematics. Each story is followed by questions and issues generated by other educators about the story. The intent of these is to prompt further thought and discussion.

Mathematics—what should we tell the children?
http://www.edfac.unimelb.edu.au/DSME/TAME/DOCS/
      TAME_RES_II.html

This site offers an interesting article by Kaye Stacey of the Department of Science and Mathematics Education, University of Melbourne, about the issue of using technology (computers and calculators) to teach mathematics. The article is informative, stimulating, and relevant to teachers from K–12. Secondary teachers might be further interested in a link to a site that concerns a teacher's experiences using Maple.

The Mathematics Projects
http://www.ed.hawaii.edu/

This site is sponsored by the Research & Development Group, University of Hawaii. The site offers access to teacher in-service programs, newsletters, and algebra, geometry, and middle years projects that reflect the NCTM *Standards*.

E-MAIL MATH
http://calvin.stemnet.nf.ca/~elmurphy/emurphy/math.html

This site provides an article describing a reform-based enrichment project entitled "Cross Cultural Story Problems in Math." The grade 4 students received story problems from Hawaii, South Africa, New York, Israel, New Orleans,

Alabama and California, and also wrote and sent their own problems to partner classrooms from the areas via e-mail. The site also offers teachers advice on setting up projects.

Office of Educational Research & Improvement
http://www.ed.gov/offices/OERI/index.html

This site provides information on educational research and reform and links to sites covering a variety of subject areas, including mathematics.

National Standards
http://www.enc.org/professional/standards/national/

This site contains links to documents, such as *Principles and Standards for School Mathematics*, that concern national standards for teaching mathematics and science.

Math Education Reform
http://forum.swarthmore.edu/mathed/math.education.reform.html

This site provides links to a variety of sites that provide information and discussion on reform in mathematics education. For example, there are links to conferences on reform and to articles and documents about reform.

Mathematically Correct 2 + 2 = 4
http://mathematicallycorrect.com/index.htm

Not all sites on the Internet applaud the recommendations of the National Council of Teachers of Mathematics for teaching and learning mathematics. For the sake of balance, one such site, **Mathematically Correct 2 + 2 = 4**, is included here. It is devoted to, in the site's own words, concerns about the invasion of schools by the "new-new math." It provides information and opinion that presents an opposing view to the NCTM-driven initiatives in reforming mathematics education. For example, the site contains reviews of textbooks and links to programs that are not based on the NCTM standards for implementation and assessment.

INFORMATION ON ASSESSMENT

There are sites on the Internet that provide information on assessment that is specific to assessing mathematics learning or that is broader in scope. The following is a sampling of the assessment sites that are available.

Other Middle Grades Resources

Assessment and Evaluation:
Resources on the Internet

To suggest additions to this list or to report bad links,
e-mail us at MiddleWeb@middleweb.com

Everything About Assessment on the Internet UPDATED

An index to just about every resource on the Internet that addresses assessment and evaluation. Fully searchable. Start here!

ERIC Clearinghouse on Assessment and Evaluation UPDATED

Basic resource for anyone exploring assessment and evaluation issues.

Tools for Accountability Project NEW!

Project by the Annenberg Institute for School Reform to promote a wholistic approach to accountability. "Accountability systems will not bring about school improvement unless they include two [critical] elements: the will and the capacity of schools to analyze data and to use that analysis to improve their practices. In addition, effective accountability must involve stakeholders outside of the school building, fostering the development of a rich reciprocal relationship between schools and their publics."

Eric Digest on Performance Assessment NEW!

A brief overview of the topic with suggested resources. Also see "A Long Overview on Authentic Assessment" written by two ERIC consultants.

Courtesy of MiddleWeb, 2000

Assessment and Evaluation: Resources on the Internet
http://www.middleweb.com/Assmntlinks.html

This site provides an annotated list of links to sites that concern assessment. Some sites are specific to mathematics while others concern assessment in general or other subject areas.

Assessment
http://www.ncrel.org/sdrs/areas/as0cont.htm

This North Central Regional Educational Laboratory (NCREL) site provides extensive information on assessment and addresses such topics as "ensuring equity with assessment" and "integrating assessment and instruction in ways that support learning." This site also provides links to other assessment sites.

NAEP Focus on Mathematics
http://nces.ed.gov/nationsreportcard/math/math.asp

This National Assessment of Educational Progress (NAEP) site provides extensive information and results on the 1996 NAEP-administered mathematics assessment of U.S. students in grades 4, 8, and 12. It also provides information on future assessments.

Mathematics Blueprint for Success
http://www.state.sc.us/sde/test123/mathbp/index.html

This site provides K–8 teachers information for preparing students for the Palmetto Achievement Tests in Mathematics.

Exemplars K–12
http://www.exemplars.com/

This commercial site offers classroom-tested standards-based assessment materials. Each of the exemplars is keyed to national standards and includes rubrics and annotated benchmark papers. The exemplars include information on time needed and interdisciplinary connections.

Mathematics Portfolios
http://users.anderson.edu/~roebuck/portassess.html

This site is a compilation of information and links that concern the use of portfolios to assess mathematics learning.

Third International Mathematics and Science Study
http://nces.ed.gov/timss/

This site provides information and data on the 1995 and information on the 1999 international mathematics and science achievement study focusing on results from the United States.

Mathematics Assessment Resource Service
http://www.nottingham.ac.uk/education/MARS/

This site is devoted to providing U.S. districts and states assistance with performance assessment design and implementation, and on professional development for designers and teachers. The aim is to help the local leadership develop local capability to meet local needs.

SMARD Website
http://smard.cqu.edu.au/

This Australian site provides substantial assistance with assessment at the secondary mathematics level. It offers teachers in-depth assessment information and resources. Most of the materials have been tested in classrooms, and much of it is nontraditional. A teacher can browse through the collection and can also contribute to the database.

COLLABORATION

Teachers sharing concerns and exchanging ideas with each other can be a powerful professional development experience. They can collaborate on projects and participate in discussions about common issues and curricula. They can talk to each other via e-mail, bulletin boards, and newsgroups. The following sites provide opportunities for such collaboration.

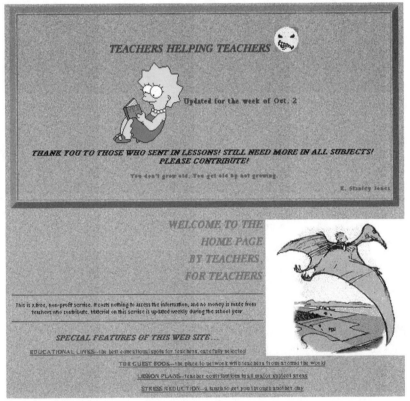

Courtesy of Teachers Helping Teachers (Scott Mandel)

TEACHERS HELPING TEACHERS
http://www.pacificnet.net/~mandel/index.html

This site offers several teaching resources, one of which is lessons submitted by other teachers. The site also offers an important professional development service, a forum for experienced teachers to share their expertise and tips with colleagues around the world.

Project Center
http://www.eduplace.com/projects/index.html

This is a Houghton Mifflin site that provides teachers with an opportunity to participate in collaborative projects in mathematics, science, reading, and social studies. On-line projects are available for perusal and participation. The site makes it fairly easy for teachers to collaborate in doing classroom projects through the Internet.

The Math Forum: Teachers' Place
http://forum.swarthmore.edu/teachers/

This site offers K–12 teachers an opportunity to join discussion groups, to ask questions, and to share their expertise with others. It also provides extensive teaching resources and links to resources.

E-MATH
http://www.ed.gov/pubs/emath/

This site provides information on and links to programs that promote collaboration through telementoring, question and answer via e-mail, and other e-mail based assistance. The links provide access to professionals who can serve as mathematics learning resources to students and teachers.

ePALS
http://www.epals.com/

This site is dedicated to helping teachers and students from around the world connect and interact with each other by e-mail and other forms of electronic communication such as voice, video or chat. The ePAL database contains tens of thousands of profiles submitted by teachers, parents and group leaders who are interested in establishing an ePALS e-mail exchange project with other members.

Title: Educational Newsgroups
http://www.edunet.ie/resources/newsgroups.html

This is a teacher collaboration site that is devoted to helping teachers communicate with other teachers through newsgroups. For example, if you are having difficulty teaching a particular mathematics concept you could post your request for assistance on a mathematics teachers' newsgroup and wait for someone to reply to your message.

CLEO: Collaborative Learning Environments On-line
http://cleo.terc.edu/cleo/cleo-home.cfm

This site supports inquiry and collaboration in science and mathematics by publishing classroom investigations on the Internet. It offers teachers access to a library of classroom projects published by classroom authors, an opportunity to join a collaborative project to share and analyze data with others, and an opportunity to publish an inquiry project from your classroom or design a collaborative project others can join.

Teacher-to-Teacher Collaboration
http://teachnet.edb.utexas.edu/~lynda_abbot/teacher2teacher.html

This gateway site provides links to sites that support teacher-to-teacher collaboration, which is focused on professional development of teachers, by teachers, and for teachers. There are some links as well to sites that foster classroom project-oriented collaborative exchanges between teachers.

GENDER CONCERNS

Women historically have been underrepresented in careers involving science and mathematics. The following sites provide resources and information that will help address that issue.

Biographies of Women Mathematicians

Welcome to the web page for biographies of women in mathematics. These pages are part of an on-going project by students in mathematics classes at Agnes Scott College, in Atlanta, Georgia, to illustrate the numerous achievements of women in the field of mathematics. There are biographical essays or comments on most of the women mathematicians and some photos (which look best at more than 256 colors). Our goal is for this list to continue to expand, and for more biographies to be completed.

We also welcome contributions of biographical information or essays from those outside Agnes Scott College. If you are interested in contributing an essay, please send your contribution to Larry Riddle. Comments, suggestions, or corrections can also be sent to this address.

ABC Names in Alphabetical Order

1718 Names in Chronological Order

Other Resources

Photo Credits

The First Ph.D's in Mathematics by Women before 1930

Prizes, Awards and Honors for Women Mathematicians

Courtesy of Department of Mathematics, Agnes Scott College

Biographies of Women Mathematicians
http://www.scottlan.edu/lriddle/women/women.htm

This site provides extensive biographical information on women mathematicians and photos of some of them as well. The site also includes links to other resources on women mathematicians and scientists.

Women And Mathematics Information Server
http://www.mystery.com/WAM/

This site provides links to information on women in mathematics, information on the WAM program and events, and an opportunity to contribute comments on women in mathematics.

Exploring Your Future in Math and Science
http://www.cs.wisc.edu/~karavan/afl/home.html

This site is part of a final project for a Women's Studies course at the University of Wisconsin at Madison. The site explores the reasons why women are less likely to enter professions in math and science, and discusses how beneficial it would be for society and the advancement of women if more women were involved in mathematics and science enterprises. It offers information on salaries for mathematics and science-related careers and on how to start a science or math club for girls. It also contains extensive links to resources for women in science or mathematics and listservers that make it possible to participate in e-mail discussion groups on gender issues in mathematics and science.

CRPC GirlTECH Home Page
http://www.crpc.rice.edu/CRPC/Women/GirlTECH/index.html

This site is not specifically devoted to gender issues in teaching and learning mathematics. Rather, its focus is girls being shortchanged in computers and technology. Some would argue that the issues are the same. The site provides some links to sites that are more mathematics-related but that still concern gender issues.

Ingear: Integrating Gender Equity and Reform
http://www.coe.uga.edu/ingear/

This site offers a toolkit of curriculum materials designed to help mathematics teachers address gender issues in the classroom.

Colormathpink
http://www.colormathpink.com/

This site is devoted to removing the mathematical barriers that prevent girls from participating in careers that involve mathematics and science. The site offers a variety of services, including homework help, information on careers involving mathematics and science, and links to mathematics resources.

Weaving Gender Equity into Math Reform
http://www.terc.edu/wge/

This site provides assistance to staff developers, curriculum writers, and workshop leaders in expanding the equity content of their workshops, videos, and written materials for teachers. It also provides assistance with multicultural and minority groups issues.

Teaching Mathematics Effectively and Equitably to Females
http://eric-web.tc.columbia.edu/monographs/ti17_index.html

This site provides information on how girls are treated in school and proposes ways to increase their interest and achievement in mathematics.

AWSEM
http://www.awsem.com/

This Advocates for Women in Science, Engineering, and Mathematics (AWSEM) site provides a variety of resources, including a newsletter, bulletin board, and links to resources for women such as information on scholarships and grants.

Women in Mathematics: Resources and Other Useful Stuff
http://camel.math.ca/Women/

This site provides information and links of interest to women in mathematics and women contemplating careers involving mathematics. Links are provided to books, articles, and speeches.

Girls: Math and Science Achievement
http://www.maec.org/girlmath.html

This site provides information on gender issues and trends. There are links to related sites and listings of available print materials.

Closing the Gap Home Page
http://www.terc.edu/mathequity/cg/html/cg-home.html

This site provides extensive information on using math clubs for girls as a way of closing the gender gap in mathematics learning. The information includes ways to start math clubs for girls and evaluations of such math clubs. The site also provides links to sites that concern gender issues.

Women in Math Project
http://darkwing.uoregon.edu/~wmnmath/

This site provides an extensive collection of links to sites dealing with gender issues including links to associations of interest to women in mathematics and links to data on the role of women in mathematics.

MULTICULTURAL AND MINORITY GROUPS CONCERNS

Mathematics is a human endeavor that is not the exclusive domain of any one culture or group of people. Yet minority groups have been underrepresented in careers that involve mathematics and science. That issue should be addressed. Today's classrooms have students of diverse cultural backgrounds. The contributions of their cultures to mathematics should be reflected in mathematics curricula. Instructional practices should pay attention to the ways in which culture may affect mathematics teaching and learning. The following sites provide information and resources to address these issues.

Mathematicians of the African Diaspora CONTENTS	
The Greatest Black Mathematicians	Profiles of ALL Black Mathematicians
Black RESEARCH Mathematicians	BLACK WOMEN in Math Sciences
A MODERN HISTORY of BLACKS IN MATHEMATICS	
AMUCHMA Online - History of Mathematics in Africa Newsletter	
The ANCIENTS in Africa	Modern OUTSIDE North America
Black and U.S. Minority Science Organizations	
COMPUTER SCIENTISTS & PHYSICISTS of the African Diaspora	Historically Black Mathematics **Departments Online** **Africa, Caribbean, & United States**
32 SPECIAL ARTICLES	NEW PHDs
Related LINKS	Statistical stuff
Sources:REFERENCES modern & ancient	SEARCH this website
AIMS, AWARDS, Acknowledgements	latest award: Acknowledged in Science 3/17/ 2000

Courtesy of Scott W. Williams

Mathematicians of the African Diaspora
http://www.math.buffalo.edu/mad/madindex.html

This site is designed to exhibit the mathematical accomplishments of the peoples of Africa and the African diaspora within the mathematical sciences. It provides information and links on black mathematicians, a history of blacks in mathematics, and mathematics in ancient Africa (other than Egypt).

Multicultural Perspectives in Mathematics Education
http://jwilson.coe.uga.edu/DEPT/Multicultural/MathEd.html

This site is sponsored by the Department of Mathematics Education, University of Georgia, to further the understanding of multicultural perspectives in mathematics education. It offers links to related sites and resources on multicultural perspectives for mathematics educators. The intent is to promote interest in teaching mathematics in a way that reflects the contributions of many cultures.

Equity
http://www.enc.org/topics/equity/

This Eisenhower National Clearinghouse site offers materials, information, and links that address equity issues in many subject areas, including mathematics.

Muticultural Math Fair
http://forum.swarthmore.edu/alejandre/mathfair/mmflinks.html

This site provides links to sites that contain multicultural resources that can be useful for teaching mathematics. For example, there is a link to a site that provides information on Mesoamerican cultures (such as the Aztec), and one that provides information on Navajo art. This information can be useful for teaching geometry.

Multicultural Learning Resources
http://www.mpls.k12.mn.us/MCGFDA/mcgfda.page7.html

This site provides information on available print and video materials that concern multicultural mathematics education.

Key Issues—Minorities and Mathematics
http://forum.swarthmore.edu/social/math.minorities.html

This site provides links to a variety of sites that concern minorities and mathematics. For example, there are links to African American mathematicians, conferences for African American educators, and Hispanic and Native American resources.

International Study Group on Ethnomathematics
http://www.rpi.edu/~eglash/isgem.htm

This site provides information on ethnomathematics and extensive links to related sites. For example, there are links to mathematics and economics sites and to critiques of multicultural mathematics sites.

Ethnomathematics
http://www.cs.uidaho.edu/~casey931/seminar/ethno.html

This site provides information on what the term "ethnomathematics" means. It also provides information on print resources for ethnomathematics and a few links to related sites.

Multicultural Mathematics and Science
http://www.uncg.edu/edu/ericcass/diverse/digests/ed380295.htm

This site contains an in-depth article (ERIC Digests on Cultural Diversity: ED380295) that discusses multicultural education in relation to teaching mathematics. The article includes an extensive bibliography.

Native American Geometry
http://www.earthmeasure.com/

This site provides information on the role geometry plays in native art and on teaching resources for teachers.

CHAPTER SUMMARY

This chapter provides information on a range of professional development websites. The resources at these sites offer opportunities for teachers to participate in professional development activities, including sharing ideas and concerns with other teachers, reading articles that pertain to reform in mathematics education, obtaining information on gender issues, and increasing awareness of minority and multicultural perspectives on teaching mathematics. Professional activities like these are as close as a URL and the click of a mouse.

APPENDIX A

Electronic Journals

Classroom Compass
http://www.sedl.org/scimath/compass/

This site provides access to the electronic journal *Classroom Compass*, which contains a collection of ideas, activities, and resources for teachers interested in improving instruction in science and mathematics.

Communications in Visual Mathematics
http://www.maa.org/news/cvm.html

This site, sponsored by the Mathematical Association of America, provides articles that cannot be presented adequately in text format, either because they rely extensively on animations and interactive demonstrations, or because they make use of hypertext features with multiple linking and nonlinear structure.

Creative Classroom Online
http://www.creativeclassroom.org/index.html

This site for K–8 teachers provides articles selected from past issues of the hardcopy magazine *Creative Classroom*.

Educator's Toolkit
http://www.eagle.ca/~matink/

This site includes a monthly newsletter that features reviews of educational websites, themes, and lesson plans, and provides resources for parents and teachers.

International Journal for Mathematics Teaching and Learning
http://www.ex.ac.uk/cimt/ijmtl/ijmenu.htm

This site provides an electronic journal that seeks to enhance mathematics teaching through relevant articles and information from around the world.

International Newsletter on the Teaching and Learning
of Mathematical Proof
http://www.didactique.imeg.fr/preuve/

This site offers an electronic newsletter published every other month, dedicated to the teaching and learning of proof in mathematics. It is intended for secondary and postsecondary mathematics educators.

Journal of Statistics Education
http://www.amstat.org/publications/jse/

This site provides access to an electronic journal devoted to the improvement of statistics education at all levels, including primary, secondary, postsecondary, postgraduate, continuing, and workplace education.

JRME Online
http://www.nctm.org/jrme/

This site provides the on-line version of the NCTM journal, *Journal for Research in Mathematics Education.*

Martindale's: Mathematics (Journals & Preprints)
http://www-sci.lib.uci.edu/~martindale/GradMath.html#JOURNAL

This is a gateway site to journals, dictionaries and encyclopedias involving mathematics.

Mathematics Teacher Online
http://www.nctm.org/mt/mt.htm

This site provides a sample of the articles found in the NCTM 9–12 journal, *Mathematics Teacher.*

Mathematics Teaching in the Middle School
http://www.nctm.org/mtms/mtms.htm

This site provides a sample of the articles found in the NCTM 5–8 journal, *Mathematics Teaching in the Middle School.*

Teaching Children Mathematics
http://www.nctm.org/tcm/tcm.htm

This site provides a sample of the articles found in the NCTM K–6 journal, *Teaching Children Mathematics.*

The Algebra Times
http://www.algebrawizard.com/

This site offers a monthly on-line newsletter that concerns teaching algebra.

APPENDIX B

The Internet Language

The Internet has its own special language. An understanding of this language is an asset for easy surfing and communicating.

American Standard Code For Information Interchange (ASCII) is a computer code that uses numbers to represent text, punctuation, and numbers.

Animated GIF is a web graphic that is animated by combining several GIF graphics in one file and playing them in sequence. It does not require special software to see the animation.

Attachment is a file that is attached to an e-mail message so that the file can be transferred via e-mail. An e-mail message cannot carry a virus but an attachment can.

Bandwidth is a measure of how much data a modem can transfer from one location to another. Bandwidth indicates the quantity of information that can be transmitted or received.

Baud is a measure of the speed of data transmission. It indicates the number of **bits** per second that a modem (for example) can send or receive.

Binary hexadecimal (Binhex) is a file that has been converted from a non-ASCII file format to an ASCII file format. This file is usually used for e-mailing because some e-mail software cannot read non-ASCII files.

Bit is the smallest unit of memory storage in a computer. In human terms, a bit can store either a one or a zero.

Bot, short for robot, is a computer program that performs an automatic function on the Internet, such as indexing web pages for search engines.

Browser is a software application used on the Internet to view and extract resources from web pages. Two popular browser programs are Netscape Communicator and Microsoft Explorer.

Byte is made up of 8 **bits.** A byte is the basic unit of memory in a computer. A kilobyte is 1024 bytes. A megabyte is 1024 × 1024, or 1,048,576 bytes.

Cache is a web browser component that temporarily stores downloaded web pages. If the web page is reloaded it displays much faster from the cache than it would if it had to be re-downloaded from the Internet.

Common Gateway Interface (CGI) is script-based software, usually written by programmers in Practical Extraction and Report Language (PERL), that instructs a web server to carry out certain operations. CGI programs/scripts usually are put into a directory called "cgi-bin."

Computer virus is a small program that replicates itself and performs undesirable actions such as erasing files and consuming all available memory.

Cookie is a small text file sent from a server and stored on the user's computer. They are used most often for customizing the appearance of web pages and keeping track of items in a shopping cart.

Cyberspace is a term coined by William Gibson. It describes the world of the Internet that carries a huge amount of informational resources through computer networks.

Domain, also known as DNS (Domain Name System), personalizes every computer in the world on the Internet. It gives a computer a number or word identification. **www.altavista.com,** for example, is a unique DNS. No other computer has that DNS.

Downloading is copying data (text, software, graphics) from the source server to another computer on the network.

Electronic-mail (e-mail) is a way of sending text messages (and graphics through attachments) across the Internet from one computer to another.

Electronic Bulletin Board System (BBS), or electronic bulletin board, is an on-line "get-together" system for people to share resources and ideas. Posting a message on one is something like posting a message on a telephone pole for a passer-by to see. A BBS system is hosted by an individual or a group.

Encryption is encoding a file to protect it from being read by unauthorized parties.

Frequently Asked Questions (FAQ) is a place where people can look up answers to much-asked questions on a particular subject of interest.

File Transfer Protocol (FTP) is a method used to transfer files from one computer to the other.

Firewall is hardware or software designed to prevent Internet users from accessing private areas of computer networks that are connected to the Internet. A firewall blocks access if security criteria are not met by the user.

Graphics Interchange Format (GIF) is a graphic file formatted into a GIF classification. Many of the Internet graphic files are in the GIF format. Another popular graphic format is **JPEG**, which is a compressed graphic file.

Hacker is a slang term for someone who breaks into computer systems without permission.

Home page is the top-level web page for a site. It normally provides links to other web pages contained at the site.

HyperText Markup Language (HTML) refers to a computer scripting language used for the Internet. HTML is used to format and lay out web pages. HTML documents usually can be recognized by their htm or html extensions (e. g., **guide2.html**).

Hyperlink is text (typically blue underlined text) or a graphic that can be linked to other documents by the click of a mouse.

HyperText Transport Protocol (HTTP) is used on the Internet to locate and retrieve multimedia files, which can contain text, sound, graphics, or movies.

Internet Protocol Number (IP Number) is a number used to identify a computer on the Internet. An IP number on the Internet is equivalent to a social insurance or social security number.

Internet Service Provider (ISP) is an organization that provides access to the Internet for a price.

Intranet is a private, local information-based network. No "outsider" can

retrieve data from this network. Its resources are available only to the members of the organization.

JAVA is a programming language for creating small applications suitable for running over the Internet. It is a language that can run on any computer, regardless of its operating system.

Local Area Network (LAN) is a computer network that is limited to a specific site or building.

Listserv is a mailing list that belongs to a group of people with the same interest. Members can share ideas via e-mail.

MP3 is an **MPEG** format used to compress audio files. Because MP3 files are small, the format has become popular for transferring music and songs over the Internet.

MPEG is the standard format for digital video compression. MPEG is short for *Moving Pictures Experts Group*.

Multipurpose Internet Mail Extensions (MIME) is used as a standard to include non-ASCII files in e-mail messages. Examples of non-ASCII files are sound, movie, and graphic files.

Newsgroup is a service provided for Internet discussions via e-mail. You can post messages on "news" computer systems. There are many newsgroups on the Internet.

Point-to-Point Protocol (PPP) enables a computer to initiate a normal connection (TCP/IP) through a modem and a telephone line to connect to the Internet.

Plug-in is a small program that "plugs into" a larger computer program to add additional features or functionality. For example, one type of plug-in enables a web browser to display multimedia files.

PDF (Portable Document File) is a file format that captures formatting information from a variety of desk-top publishing programs, enabling the documents created by those programs to appear over the Internet exactly as intended.

Protocol is an agreed-upon format for exchanging a specific kind of information between two computers. Protocols enable different computers and programs to "talk" to each other.

Server is a computer that initiates and relays all sorts of computer services,

such as sending files, to network client computers.

Shareware is copyrighted software that is distributed on the honor system. Users can try the software, and if they decide to keep it, they can send a fee to the developer of the software.

TCP/IP (Transmission Control Protocol/Internet Protocol) is the standard protocol for connecting computers on the Internet.

Uniform Resource Locator (URL) is the standard syntax to locate any resource available on the Internet. It is the equivalent of an address for a web site. An example of a URL is **http://www.uwinnipeg.ca/**.

World Wide Web (WWW) is a subset of the Internet, consisting of HTML files stored on servers that are linked to other HTML files via hyperlinks.